Why is it that my kite won't fly?

The Power of Strategic Project Management

Roberto Rodriguez Esteves

 **FriesenPress**

Suite 300 - 990 Fort St
Victoria, BC, Canada, V8V 3K2
www.friesenpress.com

Table of Contents

I dedicate this book to my parents, Oscar and Mireya—my lifelong inspiration. They have been an excellent example of sacrifice and perseverance, opening a world of opportunities for me with their hearts and intelligent advice.

Acknowledgements

Gratitude is what I feel for those who have believed in me. Whether co-worker or subordinate, you allowed thoughts and strategies to come together to make wonderful things and execute challenging projects. I am sure that, through our collaboration, many success stories are being shared. Several plants operate as expected in different parts of the world where life decided we would cross paths; our practical examples of "good work" will pass in time but will be long remembered. I'm proud to say it was through team effort, communication, trust, and leadership that we were able to complete those projects while meeting or exceeding targets. I owe much to all of you for your support.

Special thanks to my friends and colleagues: Domingo Zambrano, Jose Lotito, Miguel Guia, Elena Brey, Lorenzo Fernandez, Maria Chiquinquirá Alvarado, Antonio Saura, Ebert Cabrera, Aura Rivas, Luis Martinez, Maigualida Manzano, Jorge Morales, Manuela Fini, Efrain Moreno, Franco Del'Ovo, Esther Abreu, Heath Langemann, Luis Pereira, Gulshan Dua, Gabi Balan, Minoo Razzaghi, and the many others with whom I have had the pleasure of sharing working experiences. Together, we have done a great job!

During my professional life, I have been blessed to work for or alongside a few individuals who have inspired me to continue my quest for excellence and growth, while showing no interest in receiving anything in return. These people have acted out of pure desire to help. Whatever the reasons, I am extremely grateful for their support and advice. These incredible individuals that God put in my path are:

Gordon Finlay: In a year when I had no remote idea I would end up living in Canada and would become a Canadian citizen, I met Gordon Finlay (a Canadian and U.S. Citizen). He opened doors for me, provided me with training in non-destructive testing and inspection, and solicited a permanent residency in the U.S.A. on my behalf. Thank you, Gordon!

Carlos Ponson: He helped me get settled while working at the Refinery of Amuay. But more importantly, he encouraged me to take post-graduate studies in Project Management. That decision was without doubt the best career decision I've made. Carlos, you were so right—Project Management was my destiny! I have now made it my profession and my passion. Thank you very much.

Gerardo Aguirre: From you I learned a tremendous amount about the construction of refinery plants. It's amazing to think back to the days when we were building the delayed coker in Amuay. I admired your technical preparation, leadership, strategies, dedication, your daily walks, how you climbed all over the place to witness construction first-hand, and your respect for safety and for others. I am thrilled to have had the opportunity to work by your side. You are a true gentleman and an excellent boss. Thanks!

Gustavo Leon: It has been such a pleasure to have had you as my supervisor on two different occasions. You were the first one to stand for me when others doubted. You managed to find the time to recognize my work and provided orientation in moments when I felt a bit lost or disappointed. Your dedication, passion, detailed analysis, clarity of speech, camaraderie, trust and advice have made a huge difference in how I have achieved success. Many thanks, my friend!

Leonard Van Betuw: You have made it possible for me to work on this project. You believed in what it means for both the Oil and Gas industry and your company. You have given me a great opportunity to materialize what I've had in my head for years. I'm thankful and hope to continue partnering in order to create lots of success stories in the years to come.

Alejandro Carvallo, Gustavo Leon, and Alex Cardenas: I would like to extend my thanks for your great and objective contribution while reviewing the Flying Kite Project Execution Model. Your constructive comments, challenges, ideas, and concepts were needed to arrive to the final product. Much appreciated!

There is one very special person who perhaps does not know how much influence she has had on my professional growth. I have read the work of several inspirational authors and professionals, such as Dr. Edwards Deming, Stephen Covey, Ken Blanchard, Doug Keeley, Richard Boyatzis, Annie McKee, and other great authors; I have also attended many conferences, seminars and courses where people from different sectors, industries, and disciplines gave excellent and inspiring speeches. However, the one author that has inspired me the most is Dr. Margarita Amestoy de Sanchez. Her teaching on critical thinking principles and cognitive learning have complemented my skills on problem solving, decision making, and effective communication. Beyond that, upon learning her story, I felt a deep affinity with her struggles during the early years in Venezuela and how once she took her project outside she was able to make it what was meant to be all along: "superb, distinctive, and effective." Many, many thanks, Margarita.

I wish to thank my three daughters: Tabatha, Valeria, and Veronica. You have been my greatest motivation. From the days that you were born until today, you have taught me so much about being a father and friend to those for whom I care about and love with all my heart. Thank you for being such good children, and for sticking to the values and principles that I was able to teach you.

Oscar, Gilberto, Liliana, Nathacha, Nathalie, and the rest of the large Rodriguez Campero and Esteves Garcia families; Lia, Valentina, Josefina, and Franco Serauto: with your support, and through many shared experiences, you have contributed to my personal and professional growth. I am proud to be part of this great family. Thank you for being so wonderful!

I would like to express my sincere gratitude to the FriesenPress team, to the editor for providing such great, complete and objective analysis. To my Account Project Manager - Brelan BoyceBre, and the rest of the team, for showing professionalism, for listening and weighing in my needs and observations as an independent publishing author. You have made the publishing of my book, a valuable, delightful and enriching experience. Thanks a lot!

Most importantly, I extend heartfelt gratitude to my soul mate, wife, partner, and friend, Giovanna. You have elected to share those up-and-down moments, always choosing to help me along the way by listening, caring, making great and direct observations, and (if I may joke a bit) excellent meals. Without doubt, we have shared intense moments throughout our nineteen years together, even when things seemed static and complicated. Our love for each other served as encouragement to see the light at the end of the tunnel. Thank you for sacrificing your time to see that our daughters and I were always well taken care of.

Chapter One: A Distinctive Approach to Projects is Born

Welcome to the fascinating world of project execution!

An idea sparks a concept, and this concept is brought to reality. From conception to fulfillment, there are many plans, large sums of money, intense days of hard work, people coming and going, obstacles and eventualities, conflicting interests, change, tons of decisions, action, completion, celebrations, and lessons. When encountering so many different, dynamic components, project execution requires strategy in order to keep everything working harmoniously.

Why didn't I choose a different profession? some would ask. The truth is that there are hardly any easy professions where you work little and progress a lot. Project execution requires strategy; it requires effective methods and tools capable of producing the desired results time after time. Many challenges, including constant change, will bombard you as project manager. It can be stressful.

Think of the times when you were successful at executing a project; what worked for you? Now, think of the things that could have been done better; think of the times when the project did not seem to have achieved its goals. What was missing? This book is all about what has been missing, if not in our minds, then in the application of methodologies and tools for managing projects. It is all about taking what is out there that works and making it better. It is about creating new tools so people can be more effective at managing and executing their projects. It is about taking the Project Management profession and raising the bar, aiming at achieving effective and more consistent performance.

I am passionate about Project Management to the point that I regard my own life as a project, or better yet, a group of projects. Since childhood, I have spent my life working with a sense of purpose where each step has taken me closer to my goals. I started to work when I was thirteen as a math tutor for our neighbor's daughter. Growing up in a large, lower-middle-class family near the beach meant I had to work for what I wanted and needed, as both Mom and Dad were working hard to keep food on the table; surf boards were not on their radar when it came to things that needed attention. But we lived by the beach and surfing was the sport most teenagers wanted to practice. After a few months, I had collected enough money to buy a used surf board, but I wanted a brand-new board which meant that I had to wait a few more months. When the time came, I asked my father to take me to Caracas to the coolest surf shop to buy my board. I felt very proud of myself when I showed up at the beach the first day with my new Rocket Fish, as it was called. It cost me 1,100 bolivars, which at the time was a lot of money. I kept the receipt for many years after that as a reminder of what's possible when I set my mind to it. After that first important achievement, I worked for my first bike, my first car, my airplane tickets to visit Mom and Dad when studying away from home, and so on. Each time, I took on a little project and executed it to the best of my abilities until the project's objective was achieved.

I have learned to plan, be disciplined, be patient at times, and work fiercely to gain knowledge and experience. I have had falls and have lifted myself again. I have been assisted by others in the fulfillment of my goals, while I have dedicated time and effort to helping others reach their own goals as well. Some say that life is a journey where the destination is what we want to make of it. Our destiny in life is somewhat unknown. There are unexpected events that can certainly take our lives in a different direction, or momentarily pause our journey from arriving to our desired destination. It takes vision, persistence, and commitment to continue on our path despite the many obstacles that life puts in front of us, and persevere until reaching what we long for. Life can also be seen as project (or multiple projects), because like a journey, a project has a finite objective and a desired destination. Though no one can assure the destiny of a project, we can certainly plan it well and effectively work toward achieving the desired objectives.

To engage in a journey where there is no planning or destination is not the same as engaging in a journey where both are present. Life as a project, like a planned journey, involves having a vision, deciding to get going (initiating), planning it well so you can be better prepared for the unexpected (planning), taking action (executing), monitoring where you are, controlling what is happening, assuring you keep on track (controlling and assuring), and knowing when you have arrived (closing), at which point you may elect to undertake the next project.

I have been fortunate enough to participate in success stories while working in project execution and management over the last twenty-four years of my life. On the other hand, I have witnessed instances when projects have headed the wrong way, making their rescue a costly and seldom-forgotten experience.

One of the first concepts I learned when I started my career in Project Management was the Project Triangle, also known as the Scope Triangle, Triple Constraint, or Iron Triangle. There are different representations of the Project Triangle out there, most of which coincide in the sides of the triangle being *scope*, *cost*, and *schedule*; others add *quality* as the fourth variable. The theory is simple: You cannot change the project's budget, schedule, or scope without affecting at least one of the other two variables.

Figure 1 - The Original Project Triangle

Some have placed *quality* in the center of the triangle, while others prefer to make it a side and place *scope* in the center of the triangle. The theory is complemented by saying that once any of the three sides changes, *quality* (being in the center) would also change. This theory has been used for years to explain the fundamentals of project management.

This is based on a cause-and-effect approach that reduces the focus to these four variables, making them unique and somehow deceiving project managers into believing that if they keep an eye on these variables, things will turn out alright. Though it may have worked to some extent, it seems to fall short of addressing several other variables or conditions typically shown in project execution. Consider the following examples:

- Scope may not necessarily change, but people and conditions may.

- Safety is an important component, yet it does not appear to be addressed, because the risk component is not present.

- People may get good at doing something, thus reducing the associated time and cost without necessarily dropping quality.

Roberto Rodriguez Esteves

- Almost anything we do requires time and money; or, sometimes nothing changes yet productivity is low due to weather conditions, inadequate supervision, poor planning, and other factors that do not appear to be considered in the triangle.

If and when applying the Project Triangle to a project which has incurred in a change that affected the project's schedule and budget, we are at the stage that we are able to quantify the impact on project cost and duration, the opportunity to reduce such impact on cost and duration, has likely passed by. In other words, when we focus our attention to the impact on project cost and schedule, we actually miss the opportunity to do something about the change to minimize its impact on project cost and duration.

While trying to explain how the scope triangle works, I realized it needed to be changed in order for the concept to make better sense, and for it to become a more effective tool. Thus the following image came to mind:

Figure 2 - The New Project Triangle

Things will change in a project from the moment of conception to its completion. Those changes will typically be associated to either *scope, people,* or *conditions.* Assuming you've put a good effort into estimating a) the budget required for a project and b) the duration of said project, the other variables can change, forcing you to adjust budget and duration.

With this understanding, before you see any change whatsoever in project budget (cost) and duration (schedule), something else must have changed. Changes in cost and schedule are always the result of something else, so why is it that the focus and effort appear to be around monitoring project cost and schedule rather than in taking action to minimize the impact of change? The answer to that question led to a new Project Triangle, the one which places cost and schedule as consequences of doing or not doing something in the presence of change.

This new approach to the old theory of the Project triangle places scope, people, and conditions in the center of the triangle, showing them as the true things that can change first. Examples would be:

- An additional compressor is requested by Operations to improve the plant's reliability (scope);

- A project manager resigns and leaves without notice (people);

- Project specifications change once engaging a vendor due to its own standards (conditions).

Each one of these changes could seriously impact the project. We have an opportunity to deal with these changes, and it all starts with the application of change management in the true sense of managing the change, rather than to adjust the budget and schedule. Therefore, it is *change* that makes the first side of the triangle.

Once the change is acknowledged as needed, an evaluation of the risks associated to such change should take place. This is done to assure that we fully understand the impact of the change, not only with regard to cost and schedule, but more importantly to other direct and equally important variables, such as:

- the safety and health of personnel and other people involved in the project,

- the quality of products and services being produced, and relationships with stakeholders,

- the application of sound processes and standards, and the ability to attract or retain vendors and contractors,

- the ability to meet regulatory requirements and protect the environment,

- the potential impact on the project schedule and budget.

This is why I have chosen *risk* as the second side of the triangle.

If we think of *quality* as the mother variable that embraces everything we do, one could argue that when a change is introduced into a project, there is a risk that the quality of safety, the quality of health and motivation of personnel, the quality of the products and services, the quality of the vendors or contractors that are hired and retained, the quality of our project execution strategy, the quality of the programs (among others) may also change for better or for worse. That makes *quality* the third side of the triangle.

If the three sides are *change, risk* and *quality*, then change management, risk management, and quality management are all critical; they must therefore be visible. Rather than making it a static triangle, let us think of it as rotating clockwise (as a mechanical engineer, I tend to add motion and find the mechanics of things). The bearings that would make it rotate are precisely *change, risk* and *quality management*.

The triangle, now in motion, will rotate smoothly so long as one of the sides of the triangle is not affected much more than the other two—that is, if we introduce a change and fail to manage the associated risks and the potential drop in quality, the consequences are that those two sides could vary much more, forcing the triangle to have unequal sides, thus not able to rotate in a smooth fashion.

Like any good wheel, it needs a good tire in order to ride smoothly. In my model, the tire is like a bicycle tire composed of a rubber casing and the tire itself. Think of *schedule* and *budget* as if they were the rubber casing and the tire of the wheel, respectively.

We all know that these variables are defined early in the project and tend to be finite. That is, all tires come for a specific use and should be inflated as per manufacturer's specifications.

Now, imagine for a moment that you try to ride your bicycle with tires that are half inflated. What is the effect of this? Well, you likely won't go too fast, you will consume much more energy, and will expend more effort to arrive at your destination. This is the same effect that you see when projects are expected to be completed in a duration that makes no sense, or are given a low budget.

On the other hand, imagine now that you inflate your tires too much. The end result could be that they burst. This is the same effect that is present in project execution—that is, schedule and budget can only stretch so much before the project's benefits start to diminish, and the customer decides to stop it or remove it from those who are managing it.

The tires could also be worn out; they may have lost most of their grip and are more susceptible to getting punctured by any sharp object. This is equivalent to starting your project with little contingency. Any small event could easily create trouble and potentially make the project fail.

The new scope triangle theory is much more robust. It places the focus around change, risk, and quality, adds motion, and treats cost and schedule as consequences.

Let us now test it against the three examples described above:

In the first example, a root cause analysis may be required to identify the justifications for the *change* of incorporating a second compressor into the design. If validated, a different level of *risk* is introduced into the project. Risks such as not receiving the second compressor in time for installation, making mistakes while performing the interconnecting engineering and design, vendor getting gritty and wanting a lot more money for the second compressor, etc. may appear. No matter what, the risk level will vary with the introduction of the change. The *quality* of the plant, on the other hand, has just improved as more reliability has been added. However, if the second compressor is rushed through fabrication to meet deadlines that were not present at the beginning of the project, the quality of the second compressor may be compromised. The consequences in cost and schedule are quite obvious in this example: the cost and time of a new compressor with engineering, fabrication and installation, plus potential delays to the project to accommodate the fabrication of the new equipment piece.

In the second example, the project manager resigns without notice, which causes continuity to be broken due to a *change* in key personnel within the project organization. As a result, *risk* of delays, claims, conflict, demotivation of the team and other stakeholders is higher. The *quality* of decisions and direction during the transition period (and until a new project manager is appointed) is questionable. Special intervention by upper management may be required to avoid or minimize the impact of the project manager's absence. At the end, a potential impact in the cost of the project may result, if the replacing project manager has to be recruited outside the organization (advertising, recruiting effort, negotiating a potentially higher compensation package, mobilization of the new project manager, etc.). The schedule may be affected if decisions are postponed, morale drops, and productivity drops with it, etc.

A *change* of specifications forced by a vendor, due to its own inability to comply with customer requirements, and/or due to following less stringent standards of its own, may immediately affect the *quality* of the product being purchased. An example could be a vendor who wants to apply one coat of paint, 0.035 mm thick, versus two coats being specified by the customer. This action, if accepted by the customer, may lead to more frequent maintenance of the affected equipment piece, and increase the *risk* of having to replace the equipment at an earlier date due to corrosion. Cost and schedule may not be affected for the project itself, as no reduction in cost may be granted by the vendor, and fabrication will be completed as per the agreed schedule. However, this change may have consequences during the operation time of the equipment (more frequent maintenance, corrosion issues, and potential early replacement of the equipment). The impact is transferred from being a Capital Project Expense (CAPEX) to an Operating Expense (OPEX).

The following table shows the two levels of consequence that a change produces in a tabular form, for ease of comprehension. The two examples shown are the PM resignation and a vendor filing for bankruptcy in the middle of an existing purchase order for the project.

The analysis around change, risk and quality is typically done first; an action plan is developed, and only then cost and schedule's impact is quantified. In other words, *change*, *risk*, and *quality management* and *control* take place before *cost* and *schedule control*.

Event	Primary Consequence		Secondary Consequence	
PM resignation	Change	Organizational	Schedule	Not direct or measurable
	Risk	Loss of continuity, lack of leadership and direction, decisions missed or late. Replacement is less qualified.		
	Quality	Quality of decisions, leadership and coordination.	Cost	New recruiting process, training of new PM, others
Vendor files for bankruptcy	Change	Supply of goods and services	Schedule	Measurable impact against original delivery time. Minimized with strategic involvement
	Risk	Risk of not receiving goods as per schedule. Higher risk of having quality issues.		
	Quality	Lower quality due to loss of focus and interest	Cost	Depending on our ability to cope with the change. Additional supervision, closer follow up, special measures

Table 1 - The Effect of Change in Project Execution

"What difference does it make?" you may ask.

Well, the main difference is that we transfer the focus to *change*, *risk* and *quality*, three areas of management which tend to be under-managed in troubled projects, rather than placing it on cost and schedule. The immediate effect of refocusing your attention on these variables is that you start to see the project execution world in an entirely different light. Your frustration at seeing impact on schedule and cost for not having done much to prevent it starts to disappear.

I recently attended the Project Management Institute (PMI) for the Southern Alberta chapter, and met Warren Macdonald, an individual who inspired me beyond most keynote speakers in these types of conferences. A lover of the outdoors, he had an accident while escalating a mountain in Australia, his home country; this resulted in the amputation of both legs. He is living proof of defying all odds: not only did he survive the accident— he pushed himself to get back to hiking, scaling a mountain just ten months after losing both legs, and then Mt Kilimanjaro in Africa (5,800 meters high) two years later.

During his intervention at the conference, he stated, "How you see is what you get," and "When you change the way you see the world, you change the world."

No matter how severe a crisis you are forced to live through, if you are able to see things with a different perspective, you are able to make it an opportunity rather than a negative experience. Sometimes a different focus gives you a perspective that places you at the leading edge.

When using the new project triangle, project personnel would get in the habit of seeing change, risk, and quality as paramount variables, which would increase their chances and ability to minimize the impact on the cost and duration of the related activities, thus minimizing the overall impact on the project's budget and schedule.

If we are able to get in the habit of dealing with change as a natural phenomenon—sometimes undesired but other times necessary—our world will change before our eyes, making us more prepared to deal with it; it can make our lives much easier when managing and executing projects.

Takeaways and lessons from this chapter:

- Change is truly unavoidable, thus it should be expected, planned for, and proactively managed.

- Scope, people, and conditions may change during the course of a project.

- Once change is seen as normal, it becomes easier to draft plans and programs to better manage it.

- Effective change management requires being able to question change. Justification shall always be there before acting on it.

- Changes to scope, people and conditions have a direct effect on quality and may introduce, reduce, or increase project risk.

- Failing to perform risk analysis when faced with change is a poor practice that may lead to project failure.

- Quality of things vary when changing scope, people, and conditions.

- Cost and schedule are affected when change is introduced. The impact on cost and schedule will be minimized when performing good change, risk, and quality management.

Chapter Two: Why Aren't the Kites Flying? Project Failure Continues to Rise

Projects have been executed for many centuries, almost since the beginning of our existence. Imagine when the Great Wall of China, the pyramids of Egypt, or the now ruins of Machu Picchu were being built. Would they have worked according to a schedule? Was there a budget in mind when they started? Was anyone monitoring it at all? Likely not.

For centuries, projects were executed by creative architects, engineers, and master builders. It was not until the middle of the twentieth century that project organizations started to systematically apply Project Management tools and techniques, suggesting that in order to improve execution, core engineering fields needed to come together to work as one. As a result of that, Project Management was born and quickly became recognized as a distinct discipline of management.

We have certainly come a long way since the early days of project execution, yet it has not been enough to create continuous success at it. Why? In part, it is because project execution is a complex matter. Regardless of the type of project, whether you work for a pharmaceutical company creating new drugs, or for an IT organization developing new, faster, more effective solutions for your clients, or you work for NASA developing the next generation of rockets, project execution is complex and requires special skills and abilities.

Managing projects can be even more difficult; not only do you have to converge objectives with people and strategy, but have to deal with time and money. And there is the ever-present schedule and budget that those sponsoring the projects want you to meet.

Unrealistic project schedules and budgets are often the cause of failure. For many years, societies have been competing, and with competition came the idea that "if someone can do it, we can do it, too." This may be the reason that almost every modern company wants to do projects faster and with less money. Every so often, no one has done a similar project in such time or with such a budget, but people get it in their mind that they can be the first ones to do it.

There are plenty of examples in sports that relate to projects, because sports, like projects, rely on teams to perform. Even in individual sports, such as tennis, running, and boxing, there is a team of coaches, trainers, and other specialists working behind the scenes to get the athlete to top performance. Consider the following example:

The first individual to run a mile under four minutes was Roger Bannister from the United Kingdom. In 1954, he ran a mile in 3:59.4 minutes, a mark that many thought was impossible to break. The consequence of such an incredible feat was that soon, others were able to do it as well. Ever since Roger was able to run a mile in less than four minutes, eighteen other people have done it—and with better timing. Let us bear in mind, though, that it is still a very difficult thing to do; the last time the record was broken was in 1999 by a runner from Morocco named Hicham El Guerrouj. He ran the mile in 3:46:13 minutes. Fifteen years have passed since the time the record was last broken; technologies have improved, better diets and conditioning exist today, and yet no one else has been able to run the mile faster than Hitcham.

In projects, the level of complexity, the size, the assigned team, the location, plus a bit of the unknown (risks and opportunities) are all present, making it more difficult to compare one project to another with precision. Organizations such as Independent Project Analysis (IPA) have gathered data for years, dedicating efforts to comparing companies and their projects for the purpose of creating standards, with the hope that many others would be able to accomplish the same feat—yet many fall short of meeting targets.

There are many other consulting firms who dedicate their services to help project owners and contractors develop techniques and methodologies for executing projects with greater success.

The sad story, however, is that organizations continue to fail projects much more often than successfully completing them. Recent studies show alarming stats regarding project failure:

- IBM survey in the success / failure rates of "change" projects finds; only 40% of projects met schedule, budget and quality goals; best organizations are ten times more successful than the worst organizations; biggest barriers to success were listed as people factors: changing mindsets and attitudes – 58%. Corporate culture – 49%. Lack of senior management support – 32%; underestimation of complexity listed as a factor in 35% of projects. (Source: IBM. Type of survey: Survey of 1,500 change management executives. Date: Oct 2008.)

- A study finds that 413 of 840 (49%) federally-funded IT projects are either poorly planned, poorly performed or both. (Source: United States Government Accountability Office. Type of survey: Review of federally-funded technology projects. Date: 31 Jul 2008.)

- One in six IT projects have an average cost overrun of 200% and a schedule overrun of 70%. (Source: *Harvard Business Review.*)

- The United States economy loses $50 – $150 billion per year due to failed IT projects. (Source: *Gallup Business Review.*)

- 50% of all project management offices (PMOs) close within just three years. (Source: KeyedIN.)

- Less than a third of all projects were successfully completed on time and on budget over the past year. (Source: Standish Group.)

- 33% of projects fail because of a lack of involvement from senior management. (Source: University of Ottawa.)

- The Standish Group has done more than ten years of research, collecting statistics on information technology projects; their findings have consistently painted a dismal (albeit slowly improving) picture. For example, in 2004, only 34% of the projects surveyed met the criteria for success—completed on time, on budget, and with all the features originally specified. Of the 280,000 projects surveyed that year, more than 142,000 were late or over budget and another 42,000 failed outright. (Source: US Department of Transportation, Federal Highway Administration.)

- Our 2012 data showed only 29% of respondents consistently delivered projects on-time, 33% consistently delivered on-budget, and 35% of respondents consistently delivered on scope. Compared to our 2010 Survey, this is a significant decrease in project success rates. (Source: KPMG Advisory – 2013 Project Management Survey Report, New Zealand.)

- Between 1998 and 2008, Alberta produced many massive blowout projects. On the 109 projects that were evaluated, schedule slipped 15% on average, and cost overran between 20 and 48%. (Independent Project Analysis 2010.)

Different sources, different industries, different countries, an array of years—same poor results. This is a clear sign that there is little consistency in the application of effective methodologies, and that the lessons do not appear to be learned as years of project execution pass.

I have been studying this phenomenon for years, trying to apply quality management concepts in order to understand the root causes of the constant failures and repeated mistakes, all to try to come up with strategies and methodologies that improve project execution performance.

After a thorough analysis, twenty-plus years of project execution and management experience, numerous formal or informal audits of project teams that failed to complete their projects as per established requirements, and investigating the results presented by others analyzing the same dilemma, the following reasons for project failure appear to be the most evident and repetitive:

- Unrealistic schedules and budgets, due to poor estimating methods that rely on deceiving data from previous projects, as if projects were all alike; or, project owners insisting on working to a number that they came up with by some reference, but which makes little sense. As a consequence of working to unrealistic schedules and budgets, project teams focus all their attention to meeting them, causing all kinds of issues.

- Project teams tend to focus on following procedures without necessarily understanding the associated work processes, and without altering such procedures when in the presence of change.

- Little to no quality assurance is performed by the area supervisors. Most supervisors take the approach of performing quality assurance at the end of the process, when the work has been completed, leading to rework. The concepts of quality control and assurance are interchanged and/or misunderstood. Quality is not a given, but people treat it as if it were.

- Quality audits are generally superficial and do not explore understanding of key project management concepts and best practices. Quality auditors seem to be formed from inspection and testing organizations. This is good for manufacturing goods, but when applying quality concepts in project management and execution, quality personnel must first understand and ideally be experienced in what it takes to manage a project. Only then would they be capable of performing meaningful audits that truly help the project organizations improve. The follow-up of quality audit findings hardly ever makes it to lessons learned and implemented, so as to avoid issues from recurring.

- The work is expected to be achieved through the use of tools, with little attention to the data going in, or the applicability of the tool. This is especially important for tools used to design, estimate, plan, and engineer projects.

- No accountability is established over the work processes. Project managers appear to be accountable for every work process. Though ultimately this might be the case, not delegating accountability to subject managers provides them an easy exit for when things go wrong. The blame game between departments and among members of a project organization, with all the damage that it produces, is typically evidenced.

- Leadership in project management is not always present. The true concept of leadership, not necessarily achieved by titles or positions, is not understood nor measured. Project teams sometimes work without the needed leadership and direction, creating confusion and frustration.

- Roles and responsibilities are neither clear nor properly communicated. Many project team members spend hours attending meetings and performing ineffective tasks due to not understanding what is needed of them, nor how to go about adding value to the project organization.

- Personnel turnover or unqualified personnel, which affects project execution. Little analysis is performed to understand the causes of excessive personnel turnover to try to circumvent the situation.

- Poor management of key areas like change, risk, communications, decisions, and stakeholders.

- Project scope definition is not aligned with the proposed contracting scheme. Front end engineering is not completed or properly executed, yet the project team proceeds to the next phase and/or wants to execute under a lump sum contract.

- The estimating and management of contingency are not consistent with best practices. The project owner establishes contingency prior to performing risk analysis. Contingency is used to manage change, rather than leaving it unused for unplanned events.

- Risk levels vary as we make decisions and depart from the plan. Proper assessment and adjustment of new risk level is not systematically performed.

- Change is neither planned for nor effectively managed. Change, unmanaged risks, and poor quality have a direct impact in project cost and duration.

- Customers typically try to freeze project cost and duration, creating a challenge for managing the project's execution, while taking all of the above into account.

The need to elevate performance is imminent. I tie such need, among other things, to the ability of applying quality concepts within project management and execution. Throughout my career, and due to my involvement in inspection and quality, I have had the opportunity to review, work with, and apply standards that dictate quality for different kinds of functions and disciplines—the ASTM, ASME, and ISO standards, to name a few.

Let's face it: ISO Standards are great and provide solid ground for establishing a quality management system, but they were originally created for manufacturing and operations, not for project execution. When certifying a project execution organization to the ISO 9001 Standard, challenges quickly emerge as its applicability is not as straightforward in a changing environment, where the desired product may not be clearly defined, and where there are so many other factors and stakeholders involved.

As a response to the existing challenges in applying ISO 9001 to project execution, ISO has recently introduced the ISO 21500-2012 Standard. It has been specifically written to address project management. The newly released ISO 21500-2012 defines project management as:

> "Project management is the application of methods, tools, techniques and competencies to a project. Project management includes the integration of the various phases of the project life cycle, as described in 3.10.
>
> Project management is performed through processes. The processes selected for performing a project should be aligned in a systemic view. Each phase of the project life cycle should have specific deliverables. These deliverables should be regularly reviewed during the project to meet the requirements of the sponsor, customers and other stakeholders."

The ISO 21500-2012 Standard is at the same time defined by ISO as an informative standard. A guideline that is composed of a basic conceptual structure to allow homogeneous handling of different business processes grouped together. It may be used to create management discipline. It pre-defines common deliverables to and from each business process.

ISO makes it clear that ISO 21500-2012 is a guideline or "informative standard", and therefore one cannot certify a quality management system to this standard just yet.

The definition and structure of the ISO 21500-2012 Standard are consistent with the approach given to the Flying Kite Project Execution Model. ISO has identified ten subject groups within the Standard that include *stakeholders*, *risk*, and *communication*, which are three of the five key fundamental areas of management present in the Flying Kite Project Execution Model (to be detailed later in the book).

The idea of combining project management with quality concepts has always been there for me. I spent some time studying the quality management principles defined by ISO in *The ISO 9000:2005, Quality Management Systems – Fundamentals and Vocabulary*, and in *ISO 9004:2000, Quality Management Systems – Guidelines for Performance Improvements*, in order to better understand their applicability to project execution. The eight principles are defined as:

- Principle 1: Customer Focus

- Principle 2: Leadership

- Principle 3: Involvement of People

- Principle 4: Process Approach

- Principle 5: System Approach to Management

- Principle 6: Continual Improvement

Roberto Rodriguez Esteves

- Principle 7: Factual Approach to Decision Making

- Principle 8: Mutual Beneficial Supplier Relationships

I will explain the correlation that I see for each of these principles, in no particular order, and the degree of comprehension and successful application of each of them in project execution:

Customer focus: Every project organization should have a customer focus, so the application of Principle 1 is expected to be achieved. However, many organizations fail to see that Customer Focus in projects means being aware of the internal customers as well. The internal customers are the customers of each work process required for the project to be executed. In engineering, each discipline depends on the output of the other disciplines to produce their deliverables. Interdisciplinary coordination of deliverables is a major cause of failure in engineering, and it has to do with inconsistent or lack of attention to the needs of the other disciplines (internal customers). When this happens, there is too much focus on one's own activities and deliverables rather than the creation and delivery of the overall engineering products..

Additionally, there are times when Customer Focus is confused with Customer Pleasing, which usually leads to unbalanced and unsustainable relationships; when this happens, the customer "says" and the project organization "does". This scenario leads to many problems, including scope creep, delays, a stressful working environment, and lack of motivation, which could ultimately lead to project failure.

Leadership, the second principle, should always be present in project execution. It does not take much but getting involved in several projects even as auditors, to discern a rampant lack of true leadership in project organizations. (There is more to say on this topic, so I've dedicated an entire section on leadership further on in the book.) Bear in mind, though, that true leadership starts with one's own leadership. The first kind of leadership that is vacant in some project organizations is self-leadership—and that impacts everyone in the project organization.

Involvement of people is seen by many as getting people to do what the managers want, rather than truly getting them involved and committed. What's the difference? In the first case, people may do the work but will not be involved. They won't necessarily care if the project is completed on time, within budget, or does what it was supposed to do. Accountability is all on the manager, and the consequences of any of their actions to fulfill their instructions will be the manager's responsibility. Engaging people to work on a common objective, like executing a project together, is a process that transcends the typical request of "Could you do this task for me?"; engaging people uses an approach that says, "What do *you* think we can do to get this task accomplished, and how do you suggest we proceed?" Making people part of the plan and the strategy engages and creates commitment. Most professionals want to be motivated, and there is nothing more motivating than feeling that you are part of the equation—not just a tool to get to the solution.

Mutual Beneficial Supplier Relationships implies treating suppliers, vendors, and contractors with respect, seeing them as partners for executing projects. Since a project organization and its suppliers are interdependent, building strong, mutually-beneficial relationships increases cooperation, synergy, and added value—and long-term sustainability is more easily achieved.

Many project organizations think of suppliers, vendors, and contractors as mere service providers. These project organizations draft contracts that are one-sided; they create relationships of dependency where actions are always questioned and intimidation is practiced. In other words, they create win-lose relationships. The result is that suppliers, vendors, and contractors increase their rates to cope with the risk, hide things from their clients, and lie to take advantage of the clients. A win-lose response is given in return.

The principles which seem to be more difficult to achieve though, are the next four: Process Approach, System Approach to Management, Factual Approach to Decision Making, and Continual Improvement.

Process Approach - It is difficult to follow processes when they have not been defined. Most project organizations pretend to manage their projects through the use of procedures without first establishing the work processes. This results in the creation and maintenance of hundreds of procedures, which generally people do not have time to read or seriously take into consideration, particularly in today's fast-track project environment.

Furthermore, it creates a huge challenge for those writing the procedures to have to address almost all potential projects (small to large, simple to complex, new versus brown field, type A versus type B) and all potential clients (new versus experimented, small versus large, conservative versus risk-taker, cheap versus onerous).

In recent years, I was involved in auditing the quality management systems of two large multinational EPC organizations. In both cases, their system had thousands of procedures; some had not been updated for decades, many others were obsolete, and only few were tied to properly-defined and established work processes. Upon interviewing some of the individuals working for such organizations, I learned that, with a few exceptions, personnel were only reading and applying a few procedures—only those that mattered most to them as it applied to the work they were trying to perform.

Another issue with procedures is the need to create project-specific procedures at the beginning of the project. Project organizations often spend months trying to create and publish project-specific procedures, but this increases the expense of engineering projects and causes schedules to slip before the project even starts. Sometimes, this activity is not estimated nor accounted for in the schedule, forcing engineers to use some of the hours originally meant for the development of deliverables.

A true Process Approach to project execution is seldom found in project organizations. If project organizations were to focus on identifying, documenting, teaching, and practicing their work processes, procedures would be minimized and effectiveness would surely improve.

System Approach to Management, means that the organization's effectiveness and efficiency in achieving its quality objectives are contributed by identifying, understanding, and managing all interrelated processes as a system. Unfortunately, it is often unaccomplished due to processes that are not defined, clearly understood, nor interrelated.

People are good at creating systems, spending lots of money in purchasing and implementing those systems within their companies, and then falling short of using the systems, establishing governance around them, and continuously improving them. This is a complex issue because it involves everyone in the company, and it starts with the executives. If individuals at the executive levels are not aligned and insistent upon the use of the systems, middle management and employees will always find ways to deviate from this requirement.

Consider the following when looking to purchase systems to improve management:

- Systems should respond to the company's needs and shall be fully aligned with business and organizational objectives.

- Systems are inspired by the vision of the company, thus must change as necessary to remain up to date with such vision.

- Systems require IT support, vendor support, and training of personnel to assure everyone is utilizing them to their full potential.

- Systems are normally controlled through license rights. All associated costs must be budgeted for, particularly when applied at the project level.

- People respond to systems in different ways depending on their origin, culture, language, and past experiences.

- Systems shall be selected to improve company performance, gain additional business, optimize profits, and attain sustainability. As such, they should be fundamentally aligned to the company's work processes, not the other way around.

- Systems that are well-established within the organization shall be considered part of the working culture. Governance around their mandatory use is imperative.

- Systems shall be user-friendly, simple, concise, and effective.

- An excessive number of systems, or systems that are too complex, will lead to under-utilization and employee frustration.

- Regular evaluation of systems by the company's executives, based on employee feedback, is required to assure adequate use and to promote prompt modifications or replacement, when necessary.

The third most under-utilized Quality Management principle is *Factual Approach to Decision Making*. We work hard to reach positions in management. Becoming a project manager is definitely a good step in anyone's career growth, and the experience can be both challenging and gratifying. Some people reach these positions and unfortunately forget about the basics for making decisions, as well as how important it is for the success of the project team to make informed and factual decisions.

The chart below shows different suggested steps to assure decisions are accurate, effective, and promptly made:

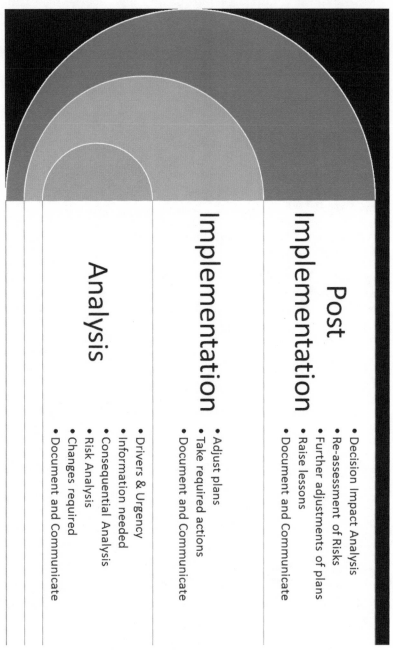

Figure 3 - Project Decisions Analysis

Roberto Rodriguez Esteves

Our decisions, when in leadership roles, can affect the outcome of our project. Yet how many organizations monitor the effectiveness of these decisions? Why not consider that important decisions in project execution need to be followed up to measure their impact and effectiveness? How do we expect to learn from past decisions if not establishing a process to measure their effectiveness?

Managers may be reluctant to have such a system implemented in their project organizations because it could reveal that decisions were not made with sufficient information in hand, while performing analysis of potential outcomes, or on a timely manner.

Until project organizations get in the habit of monitoring their decisions, little learning will result, and project failures will be blamed on other things.

The last most un-achieved Quality Management principle is *Continual Improvement*. Project organizations that fail at implementing sound practices to achieve the other seven principles stand little chance of achieving improvement, much less continual improvement. (Some of the challenges and strategies for achieving continual improvement are discussed at more length later in the book.)

In summary, we have progressed quite a bit since the days that projects were executed without guidance, tools, and methods. However, the rate of failure continues to be high and requires acting *now*. In the following chapters of the book, I will present solutions to most common issues when describing the Project Execution model I have developed (the Flying Kite Project Execution Model).

The need is there to:

- elevate our performance in project execution

- succeed in the application of quality concepts within project management and execution

- increase the knowledge and understanding of project management concepts and best practices

- build projects with the whole life cycle in mind (CAPEX – OPEX)

- meet project targets on a regular basis

- implement effective quality assurance that involves:

  a. thoroughly evaluating and upgrading the existing quality management system,

  b. applying project execution best practices,

  c. managing performance at the work process level,

  d. implementing strategies for managing stakeholders (customers) and meeting their expectations,

  e. facilitating the application of quality concepts and continuous improvement process, and

  f. setting accountability and establishing governance.

It's up to us to do something about it! It is the profession we have chosen; we must stand firm and united in our quest for solutions.

Roberto Rodriguez Esteves

Chapter Three: Fundamental Areas of Management to Get Kites to Fly Again

The Project Management Institute (PMI) and other organizations have certainly put together helpful information on key areas of learning. The Project Management Body of Knowledge (PMBOK) is an excellent standard by which to guide project teams to effective project execution. The PMI recently incorporated a new section to the PMBOK—section 13. It provides guidelines for performing Stakeholders Management. This is a great step toward taking our focus away from the traditional schedule and cost, and directs it to softer and more difficult areas of management that have become crucial for sound project execution.

Most people would agree that it is easier to learn and apply hard core subjects than it is to learn soft skills in order to establish relationships and manage human resources. Nonetheless, project management is primarily "people management", and those who are able to effectively manage people stand a better chance of completing their projects on time and within budget, while simultaneously meeting safety, environment, quality, and sustainability requirements.

Many of us did not have the opportunity to take psychology or other social studies subjects in college, so how are we expected to understand people and build the necessary relationships that would increase our success rate during project execution? How do we learn to better exert leadership, manage conflict, motivate our team, effectively recruit personnel, perform competency gap analysis, assess communications in a project, make factual decisions while engaging stakeholders, negotiate our way out of a change order, etc.

To complicate things further, the new generation of professionals appear to be more inclined and accustomed to communicating through the different ways that technology now allows, such as chatting, texting, social networks, and other media, none of which are based on direct contact with the individual with whom you are trying to communicate. There is lots of room for interpretation when one receives a text or email from another person. There is no real opportunity to read body language; true emotions may be easier to hide, making it more difficult for effective communication to exist.

Older generations of professionals, such as the Baby Boomers, are reaching retirement age. Combine this with technological advances (where face-to-face communications are no longer a necessity) with an imminent need for professionals with project management experience; factor in the record number of projects failing completion as per requirements, and it seems a perfect storm is brewing. This may have serious consequences in the decades to come unless effective counteraction is taken to minimize its impact.

To circumvent the formation of such a perfect storm, I suggest to take the following steps (though it is by no means a complete list):

- Develop a project execution system that elevates the importance of the typically hidden work processes, such as those associated to communications, decision making, and stakeholders' management.

- Make such system so that it teaches young professionals about the work processes of project management and execution, ensuring quality control and assurance is performed at the work process level.

- Redirect the focus to change, risk, and quality management as prime areas of management to create success in project execution.

- Walk away from old management styles that rely on intimidation and lack of empowerment; move toward innovative, participative, and responsibility-sharing leadership styles. Grant accountability at the work process level.

- Engage the new generation by speaking their language. Do not expect them to understand the way you were taught—make use of their intelligence, technological savviness, energy, and sharpness to create the results. Newer generations are less patient, and are much more aggressive and eager. They generally aim higher but want results right away. To keep them motivated, it may be necessary to break the project into smaller pieces, thus allowing for success and recognition to be both achieved and celebrated more often. They absolutely hate micromanagement and love multi-tasking!

- We can no longer expect to retain individuals without sound succession plans. These succession plans must be both in place and fully communicated to the personnel. Stop thinking you are in charge today; think of tomorrow. Sustainable business means caring for the people who make it happen. One of the reasons we have such a gap today in the availability of good managers is the mentality that many managers have had for decades, one that says, in effect, "I care about my career and must maintain all the knowledge I have in my brain to avoid having others substitute me." No one is indispensable. When you keep it all to yourself, even if you have a successful career, you will likely leave no legacy. Leaders who tolerate such behavior in their organizations contribute to a darker tomorrow.

- Insist on retaining good values and work ethics. Honesty, sincerity, respect, and responsibility continue to be key elements for creating a sustainable business.

- Volunteer to teach and train others as you become experienced, knowledgeable, or reach your retiring age. Spend lots of time with teenagers and other young adults to understand their language, needs, strengths, weaknesses, and points of view. Be a true leader for future generations by showing them the way (modeling the behaviors) with humility and character. Integration is necessary! Don't expect them to be the ones to reach out.

- Push yourself beyond your boundaries; teach yourself a new computer software program or application. Stay as current as possible with technology so you are able to communicate to others and identify challenges with communicating through the use of these new tools. Formulate plans to integrate such concepts into project execution.

- Be proactive in providing quality assurance and control. Eliminate fear and negative consequences to those involved in non-conformances. In Dr. Edward Deming's eight principles of management (from his book *Out of the Crisis*) he states, "Drive out fear so that everyone may work effectively for the company." Utilize the system as a tool to generate value. In order to keep the system current, people must be able to learn and improve from its own use. If such learning is not incorporated in a positive and encouraging manner, continuous improvement won't be achieved. A system without continuous improvement quickly becomes obsolete and dies, as it is not capable of adapting to change, human error, or limitations. A system is not able to correct its ineffective work processes and procedures by itself. It is the people who use it who should be both responsible and accountable for keeping the system accurate, updated and effective.

I have had the fortune of growing my professional career through exposure to many areas of the business, including maintenance and troubleshooting of equipment in the aviation industry, inspection and testing of metals and other materials, construction of large projects, project engineering, engineering management, project management, quality and HSE directing, and entrepreneurial endeavors. Through this exposure to the many angles of project execution and direction, a path for seeing things with an integrated perspective seems to have opened, allowing me to learn a great deal from directly handling issues and challenges that emerge from this array of areas and disciplines. This exposure has allowed me to formulate my own vision of what can be done better.

You can spend many years in Engineering without stepping a foot on a construction site, thus possibly never understanding the limitations of building something. The same can be said for the maintenance of the related equipment, particularly if you have not spent time starting a plant, talking to the plant operators and maintenance personnel, or have never seen a component fail during operation. It may be quite a difficult task to design the facilities while providing the necessary access for maintenance. Exposure is what provides engineers with the necessary knowledge to improve design, allowing for the introduction of constructability, operability, and maintainability concepts into the design.

On the other hand, demand for project management personnel is high, thus it is more common nowadays to see young professionals with little experience (but who may be sharp in their own area or discipline) assuming leading roles in a project organization. Unfortunately, these young professionals may lack experience dealing with the number one resource in project execution: people. It appears this situation will worsen in decades to come, so it is critical that project management be given attention while focusing on areas that are often hidden, under-managed, or undervalued.

These fundamental areas of management for successful project execution are, in my opinion: *Decisions, Communications, Stakeholders, Change, Risk* and *Quality*. This is the basis for the Flying Kite Project Execution Model. Please notice that *Schedule* and *Budget Control*, though important, are not present in the list, due to the arguments presented in earlier chapters of the book.

The Flying Kite Project Execution Model integrates these five fundamental areas of management in a work process based system, where each work process is described in detail, and where accountability for each and every work process is assigned to the most suitable individual within the project organization.

Key performance indicators are set around the work processes, thus assuring the focus is maintained at the work process level. The success of the project relies on the successful execution of these work processes. Quality is measured at the work process level through these key performance indicators, making it intrinsic to the work process.

A brief word on good quality schedules. Consider the following statement:

"All projects have a schedule!"

Not many projects, however, have a *good quality* schedule—one that has been prepared while taking into account project requirements and vendor information; has been checked by key members of the team; has been loaded and linked properly; has been tied to the project budget; is logical; is broken down to the needed level according to the phase of the project being executed; has been prepared within a reasonable time after project start; and has been distributed to all those who need to understand and work by it, and has been approved both by the project team and the customer.

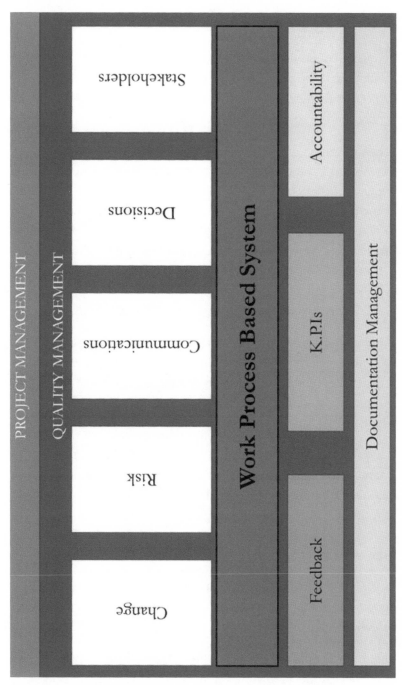

Figure 4 - The Flying Kite Project Execution Model Structure

In other words, what project organizations require to succeed is a *good quality* schedule, not just a schedule.

The same can be said for the Project Budget, the Project Execution Plan, the Scope Statement, the Project Charter, the Project Procedures Manual, to name a few project deliverables needed for the sound execution of a project.

Project execution involves many players: the owner and its organization, the project team, the contractors, the vendors, the regulators, etc. These stakeholders typically have different interests while accomplishing the same goal. At times, this can lead to conflict and occasionally to legal action. The prime activity that can assist any project team in avoiding conflict and litigation is *documenting*. Unfortunately, another major cause of project failure and claims is the lack of structured, well-kept, properly-identified, traceable and duly-archived documentation.

Many project organizations settle for informal communications, are not careful enough to set the rules of engagement for when formal communication is required, and allow people to use their personal drives to archive important project information—all of which invite trouble.

Good intentions are usually not enough; discipline is required to establish the necessary documentation management and control culture—a culture where the document controller is your best ally, the one who can help you get your project ahead, and eventually keep your project organization out of claims or legal action from other stakeholders.

The Flying Kite Project Execution Model places emphasis on documentation management and thus makes it visible to the individuals utilizing the system and managing the project.

The theory behind the structure of the Flying Kite Project Execution Model, shown in Figure 4, is simple:

- Learn and follow your work processes

- Communicate effectively

- Manage change, risk, and quality in your project as per the revised scope triangle

- Make factual decisions

- Ensure effective management of stakeholders

- Document, document and document some more

In synthesis, project management is as much a science as it is an art. A different and more effective approach is needed to improve our chances of meeting project targets in a systematic manner.

A different definition of project management would be something like this:

> "Project management is the art of managing human resources through effective leadership, sound decision making, and communications. The aim is to create something unique while taking into account risks and opportunities that appear as a result of change, and while following established work processes with quality. All of this shall be done with an estimated duration and cost in mind, while following a plan and creating the necessary records."

Now let us see how the concepts behind the Flying Kite Project Execution Model work when applied to a true example taken from a typical engineering project:

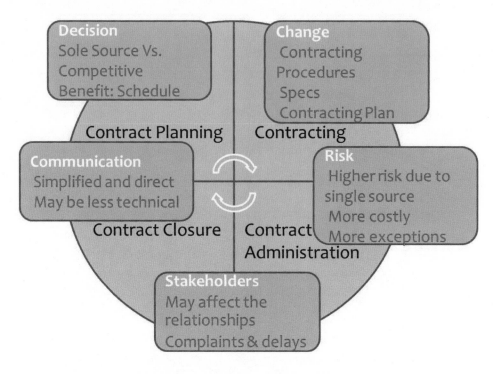

Figure 5 - A Work Process Example for
Fundamental Areas of Management

In this figure, *Contracting*—a typical process in project execution—is broken down into its execution phases: *Contract Planning, Contracting, Contract Administration and Control,* and *Contract Closure.*

The example involves a decision that is made some time into the project to deviate from standard procedures and awards a purchase order to a compressor manufacturer as single source. This implies not having to realize a bidding process, but rather awarding the purchase order based on receiving this vendor's proposal.

The decision has been supported by Management on the basis of the project being late and needing to recover some time. A change is born; thus Change Management should kick in right away.

Roberto Rodriguez Esteves

The engineers have validated that this vendor generally meets the technical requirements, so the project team will process a deviation to the established project procedures in order to award directly to this vendor.

Now, what would result from this project decision?

Let's evaluate the risks associated with this decision and the potential impact if they were to materialize:

- Other vendors may complain that they have been unjustifiably removed from the short list of vendors, not allowing them to compete for this solution.

- The selected vendor may generally meet specifications, but when engaging this vendor as a single source, the project team runs the risk of the vendor not being able or unwilling to meet all project specifications, thus forcing the project team to waive some requirements.

- The purchase order may turn out to be more costly, as competition has been ruled out.

- The vendor fabrication process may take longer than it would have for another vendor. No certainty exists that the chosen vendor can actually fabricate faster than the competition.

- If the vendor was aware of the project team's intentions of awarding this purchase order as a single source, it may try to lower the quality of certain components to reduce expenses and thus make additional profit. This may imply that the quality of the compressor ends up being inferior to what had been intended.

- The selected vendor may claim they can only proceed according to their own standards, forcing the project team to again waive certain requirements and placing them in a position to have to accept lesser quality of some or all of products being purchased.

- The lead rotating equipment engineer may disagree with the project leads (project manager or whomever is making the decision) with regard to this decision, which may lead to friction within the organization and low morale; this could ultimately lead to the engineer's resignation.

As can be seen, a simple decision, which appears to be justified, may translate into a series of risks that at the very least must be addressed and mitigated in order to avoid negatively impacting the project.

All of this would probably happen without the knowledge of key stakeholders, if the work processes associated to decision making, communications, and stakeholders' management were not well established.

Before we can even think of the impact of this change in cost and schedule, many other things need to happen. The decision should be recorded; the change needs to be communicated to the stakeholders of this work process; the risks must be analyzed; responses to these risks must be identified and documented; stakeholders must be managed.

Once these steps have been completed and a direction is given to the team on how to manage associated risks, an impact on the project schedule and the costs associated with dealing with this change are estimated.

In a perfect world, no one should work with this change until it has been duly approved and such approval has been communicated.

An idea that started as a cost- and time-saver may turn out to cost *more* time and money to implement. This is the challenge most project organizations face. The situation worsens when work processes are not established and the effectiveness of decisions is not tracked. This decision was born out of the need to shorten the schedule and thus as an opportunity. Opportunities are definitely worth pursuing. One must make sure that associated risks are identified and measured against the apparent benefits to the project that the opportunities would bring upon implementation.

Chapter Four: The Human Factor

The human factor in project execution is paramount. Even if we had the luxury of having modest project schedules and budgets, without people, projects would simply not get done.

Many project managers and directors would rather concentrate on the technical aspects of project management (e.g., creating a strategic plan, preparing budgets and schedules, writing project specifications, etc.). But at the end, it is human resources who deserve to be in the spotlight. They deserve plenty of attention to achieve good results.

Why don't we spend sufficient time dealing with people's issues? Well, likely because it's complicated, time-consuming, and seldom recognized; some even think it's a waste of time.

The following sections explain the formula that, in my opinion, is needed to make human resources our paramount resource.

People

Many declare that people are the most important resource. How many actually mean it?

People are our most important resource, but only those who are qualified and available to perform the tasks can assure the desired results are achieved from the first time around.

Our duty as supervisors is to ensure that personnel are prepared for the challenges that lie ahead by:

- Seeking individuals who are trainable and possess the best skills to succeed in the workplace.

- Selecting individuals on the basis of the best available candidate for each and every position, while evaluating knowledge, abilities, skills, experience, and personality.

- Providing adequate orientation to the employee once on board, so they have good understanding of the goals, values, standards, and best practices of the organization and how to contribute in achieving them; describing roles and responsibilities in detail to the employee, seeking their understanding and acknowledgement.

- Identifying and documenting weaknesses and strengths to allow for adequate training plans; preparing, discussing, and documenting such training plans.

- Supervising the employee while executing day-to-day activities to provide them with guidance and needed information; identifying areas requiring preventive action by either the employee or the supervisor to avoid rework, and to assure quality of work and success. Micro-management shall be avoided at all times.

- Providing encouragement and support on a regular basis. A good percentage of the employee's success is associated with the supervisor's ability to support, coach, motivate, and encourage the employee.

- Creating a positive working environment, where team spirit and collaboration is the norm. Working effectively, leading by example, being humble, listening to their ideas, delegating responsibility while assuming one's own are all key components of a positive working environment.

- Performing regular evaluations with each employee to discuss progress of personal objectives; to share each other's views on team performance, leadership, and accomplishment of organizational goals; and to go over the employee's strengths and weaknesses, as observed by the supervisor, to make adjustments for improvement and to produce modified objectives and training plans for the next evaluation period.

- Purging the organization when necessary. Employees who under-perform in their current positions, after all of the above and after consecutive evaluation periods, shall be recommended for transfer to other positions or departments within the organization. Dismissal may be necessary in cases of adaptability problems, persistent under-performance, or other severe employee issues.

- Painting a bright future for the employees by implementing adequate compensation and succession plans in the organization. Employee retention is directly proportional to having a successful and more profitable organization. Excessive rotation of personnel leads to low employee morale, a more expensive training program, lack of continuity, waste of time, frustration of both colleagues and supervisors, and the need to carry an excessive Human Resources organization.

A healthy organization is made of qualified, motivated, and experienced individuals working toward common goals. A good atmosphere is seldom a natural phenomenon, but rather the result of continued efforts by the supervisors, managers, and executives within the organization; such leadership provides support and models behavior that lead to success.

Consider the following statement: "Supervisors and managers working for employees to create a brighter and more successful organization, while employees work for the organization to make it happen."

Why is it so difficult to see this regularly happening in companies around the world?

In part, it is because working societies have taught us differently. From school age, children are generally taught to compete, which is a good thing to understand and practice, but they are hardly taught to look down and help others who reach for the rung on the ladder on which they stand. Or are they?

In organizations, people work long hours, struggle through difficult moments, fight back, patiently progress, finally make it, and then forget they themselves were ever at the bottom rung of the ladder. To make things worse, ego kicks in, and they feel it's a given to have others follow them for a change, if only by virtue of their designated authority. An attitude of "I'm better informed on what is required for the project, the team, or whatever other thing being managed" creates a barrier between the leader (supervisor, boss) and the team (supervisees, employees).

Some argue, "If I have to invest all this time making sure people under me know what to do, have the tools to do it with, are adequately supervised, and that I am opening the path for them to succeed, who is going to do my work?"

Through audits I performed, and while questioning leaders and supervisors about how much time they spent making sure their team had the right information and were using the right tools, assuring quality of their work, and providing quality control of products and services, I learned that only about 10% of the time was being spent on such activities. How could anyone expect results to be anything other than deficient under these circumstances?

This particular unfavorable situation was repeated in different groups, departments, and project organizations. Supervisors and managers were not supervising nor managing. The majority of time, this was being caused by the expectations set by the companies where these supervisors and managers work, whereby they were expected to directly produce services and deliverables for their customers. Other times, it was because the individuals who reached those positions never stopped doing the technical work for their discipline. In other words, they never left the old jobs as technical leads. A few times, this unfavorable situation was caused by indifference on the part of the affected supervisors and managers. In other words, they did not care enough to spend their valuable time helping their own teams. Occasionally, it was caused by being too busy with many simultaneous projects, leaving little time to perform adequate follow-up and supervision.

The formation of effective teams indeed takes time and effort. Spend time working for your team if you want to see them producing to the best of their potential. If not sure where or how to do it, start by opening up; gather with them and seek to describe success as seen from their perspective. Set direction but play along; be supportive and motivating. Magical things evolve from engaging people!

Communications

Issues associated with poor, insufficient, or lack of communication are another leading cause of project failure.

I consulted an article published by PMI in May of 2013 called "The High Cost of Low Performance: The Essential Role of Communications". Below are a few excerpts from this article to illustrate my point:

> "As reported by PMI's 2013 Pulse of the Profession™, an organization's ability to meet project timelines, budgets and especially goals significantly impacts its ability to survive—and

even thrive. As they address the urgent need to improve project success rates, organizations are faced with a complex and risky environment that includes:

» A "do more with less" economic climate

» Expanding global priorities

» Necessity to enable innovation

The Pulse study also revealed that *the most crucial success factor in project management is effective communications to all stakeholders*—a critical core competency to all organizations. In a complex and competitive business climate, organizations cannot afford to overlook this key element of project success and long-term profitability.

PMI's 2013 Pulse of the Profession™ report revealed that US$135 million is at risk for every US$1 billion spent on a project. Further research on the importance of effective communications uncovers that a startling *56 percent (US $75 million of that US $135 million) is at risk due to ineffective communications.*

Despite this risk, many organizations admit that they are currently not placing adequate importance on effectively communicating critical project information, especially when explaining the business benefits of strategic initiatives to stakeholders at all levels of a project. Organizations cannot execute strategic initiatives unless they can effectively communicate their strategic alignment and business benefits.

The third global PricewaterhouseCoopers LLC (PwC) survey on the current state of project management reveals that, according to executives, effective communications is associated with a 17 percent increase in finishing projects within budget.

Similarly, the Towers Watson 2011 – 2012 "Change and Communication ROI Study Report" shows that companies that have highly-effective communications practices are 1.7 times more likely to outperform their peers financially.

Not all projects succeed. On average, two in five projects do not meet their original goals and business intent, and one-half of those unsuccessful projects are related to ineffective communications."

In order for communications to be considered effective, the intended message must be received and acknowledged as comprehended. The message when fully understood must produce the desired and expected action (or reaction). When it comes to information sharing, whether it is done intentionally or unintentionally, the associated communicated is regarded as effective, again, if the people's behavior and response reflects common understanding of what is being shared. The contrary effect would constitute evidence of potential distortion of the messages during the communication process.

Effective communication not only should generate the desired effect, but should maintain the effect and potentially increase the effect of the message.

Effective communication is said to meet the following general requirements:

- Explicit, detailed and yet concise

- Timely

- While breaking all barriers

- Useful and consistent

- Factual and well supported

- Honest and sincere

- Understood and acknowledged

- Utilizing the most effective means (written, spoken, direct, telephone, web, etc.)

- Formal when need be

- Documented

Unfortunately, there are barriers to effective communication, which come in different ways, causing delays, distortion, and in cases even changing the intention of the message being conveyed. In order for communication to be effective in project execution these barriers must be overcome or diminished. There is good reading material on effective communication on the web, most of which define the typical communication barriers. I am simply going to name a few, which in my opinion are common within a project environment:

- *Physical barriers* (Example: project personnel physically located apart from each other, unable to perform face to face communication)

- *Unclear or Unexpressed Roles and Responsibilities* (lack of clarity in roles and responsibilities causes people to communicate too much, too little, or inadequately)

- *Leadership Related Barriers* (a result of poor communication of goals by the leader, inconsistent messages, lack of direction, etc.)

- *Language Barriers* (people working in a project where English is the official language, but it happens to be their second or third language)

- *Company Culture Barriers* (employees not familiar or not used to company values, not familiar with policies and standards, may make improper use of emails, may not inform those who would need to be informed, etc.)

- *Physiological barriers* (poor eyesight or hearing difficulties, among others)

- *Cultural differences* (between people who come from different parts of the world, different gender, different age, or social status)

The effectiveness of communication should be measured in a project environment, with the hope of improving our chances of succeeding at executing the projects that we undertake. The following performance indicators serve as guidelines for some of the things that a project organization can set to measure in order to validate that the work processes around communications are well established, and communications are being effective. Communications need to be:

- Managed at the work process level, and monitored at the project level,

- With clear distinction between what needs to be formal or informal,

- With norms about what must be documented and how to go about it,

- Orderly documented and archived,

- While using established, easy-to-locate, and effective forms and templates,

- While ensuring that they are multidirectional (up, down, across, diagonally) both outside and inside the organization

- Meaningful, accurate, concise

- Delivered in a timely fashion, comprehended, acknowledged and acted upon

- Measured regularly throughout the project execution

- Held within or accessible from a single system while respecting required confidentiality

- Properly supported and endorsed at the right level within the organization

Leadership

Being a leader is no piece of cake. It requires a lot of preparation, tons of commitment, great passion and a full plate of people skills seldom learned from regular school programs. So how do we know when we've got what it takes?

Well, a good start would be to look back and think of the times you were able to lead your siblings, close friends, or school mates into doing something. Yes, anything! Chances are, if you were able to lead others in an activity of interest, you started to build your leadership skills at that early stage of your life.

Another signal of possessing leadership skills lies with having met your own goals. Having a vision of life and planning to achieve it demonstrates self-motivation and self-discipline; which together with the ability to learn from mistakes are also signs of self-leadership.

Some people think that leaders must be like super-heroes: never wrong, always there, fearless and strong. It so happens that even the greatest of leaders would have made some mistakes, would have shown some weaknesses, would have required assistance, and would have been absent at one point in time or another.

Others think that leaders should be friendly, caring, sensitive to everyone's feelings, and willing to sacrifice. Compassion is a great skill to have, but leaders cannot afford to be Mother Theresa all the time. They will need to make the occasional unpopular decision, exert authority to get a task accomplished on time, or take corrective action when facing under-performance.

Leaders are expected to take the hit for people when things go wrong. When swimming in an ocean of responsibility (water) and accountability (waves), some will swim with the waves (assume accountability) and others away from them (refuse to assume accountability – want to be responsible but not accountable). Justice is hard to come by for leaders, whether they take the beating on behalf of the team (assume the accountability on behalf of those who should have), or try to place the blame on those truly accountable for the tasks that failed, which may be seen as finger pointing. Therefore, the best advice is to identify and clearly communicate who is accountable for each task (group of tasks, or work process), and enforce it. Your role is to support and coach those in your team, not to pretend that you can be accountable for everything being done. This implies that you must responsibly delegate the necessary functions so that with your guidance all necessary activities are performed.

Delegating responsibility to any individual in the organization, without also delegating the corresponding authority and control; without providing the required direction, information, and guidance; and without simultaneously allocating the implied accountability is a mistake that we as leaders cannot afford to make.

There are other fundamental aspects of Leadership, namely: courage, willingness and commitment. The courage to speak up or to take the first step; the willingness to act or to say NO when is necessary; and the commitment with themselves and those who follow them to keep on moving (maintain the inertia). Leaders take risk, are courageous, are not afraid of the consequences of failing, because they have understood that their actions and the inertia that they generate are fundamental for things to happen. Creation and innovation are not possible in status quo. Failure is treated as momentary and a great contributor to making things better in the future.

If you have become a leader, you should be proud of yourself, but you must remember that you are only half-way there. The next and more important step is maintaining and improving your leadership style and skills. Like Covey's seventh habit of highly effective people, if you do not sharpen the saw, your leadership will likely fade away. This means you must work hard at keeping up with organizational change, newly-developed techniques, and the lifestyles of new generations; simultaneously, you must modify your own leadership style and the application of associated skills to continue to influence those who follow you.

Here are some skills that, in my opinion, every leader should have:

As it relates to the task:

- Able to prioritize

- Exerts hands-on management

- Facilitates and provides resources

- Sets measurable goals

- Good understanding of risk while committing to risk management

- Consistent in providing direction

- Allows for the most knowledgeable person to lead the way

- Possesses good vision

- Open to change and new ideas

- Practices effective and engaging decision making

- Studies Situational Leadership and applies it. It is the most effective way to determine which style should be used for different situations.

As it relates to people:

- Creates trust and respect

- Stands behind the team, and acts in support of achieving set goals

- Promotes and celebrates achievements

- Coaches others

- Allows for the personal growth of others

- Engages people in decision making

- Provides incentive to those involved in a job well done

- Shares responsibility for mistakes made by the team

- Leads by example—"walks the talk"

- Transfers good values

- Helpful, caring

As it relates to the leaders themselves:

- Sincere and realistic

- Encouraged and confident

- Proactive and open

- Available and approachable

- Creative

- Good communicator

- Transparent

- Patient

- Emotionally intelligent

There are those who become leaders by popularity (charisma), others by their knowledge and wisdom, others by their vision and strategies, others by their abilities to perform at whatever discipline they are good at, and others for standing up and defeating fear. In any case, a leader needs followers—and as leaders, our duty is to the followers. We owe them respect for the trust they have placed in us, sometimes despite not knowing us well. One of the easiest ways to lose your leadership is to fail to give the same respect and trust to them. If you have accepted your role as a leader, you must now play it accordingly.

Tools

> "If the only tool you have is a hammer, you tend
> to see every problem as a nail."

People who have the necessary competency level for the job but use the wrong tools achieve poor results; thus it is vital to learn how to select tools, despite sometimes being a tedious, challenging, or frustrating task. Special attention, when selecting tools, shall be given to justification, audience, and the work process for which the tool is needed. Not having clear understanding of these variables may lead to selecting the wrong tools, having to train personnel on tools that they won't use, and paying for unnecessary license premiums.

We tend to fall in love with tools once we see all they can do, forgetting for a moment whether we even need them in the first place. A versatile and fast tool can easily impress anyone. Computer and software companies seem to compete daily in creating yet another version of their products—one that is faster, one that is brighter, one that can do it all, one that is perfect for you, only to introduce a better one just months after you got hooked on the first one. This is a great marketing strategy that keeps us (the consumers) spending our money year after year, to generate more profits for them without providing much increased benefit for us.

Don't get me wrong! I don't oppose technological advancement; rather, I'm referring to a situation that affects our budgets without necessarily providing more functionality, or enhancing the performance of the associated tasks. You can make a phone call, send an email, chat with friends, take pictures, etc. with most cellular phones nowadays, yet most people want the latest of the latest.

That same phenomenon could be seen in some companies where electronic tools seem to drive the destiny of the company. Tools change so quickly that there is insufficient time to learn how to use them or measure their effectiveness—or sometimes, tools are even selected without a sound basis. In contrast, other companies expect to resolve everything with a single tool (e.g., "All you need to manage a project is Primavera." That's like saying, "All you need to build a house is a hammer.") And other companies seem to suffer from "Blame it on the tools" syndrome, where the blame for missed targets and constant underperformance is placed on the tools. Sometimes it's true that tools could be obsolete, but more often, nothing changes after new tools are procured and applied. The cause may rest on lack of understanding of work processes, poor supervision, reactive quality assurance, etc.

Tools should be selected as a response to a specific need (e.g., to open a twenty-five-meter-deep hole in the ground to pour a pile), a specific objective (e.g., we would like to pour eight piles per day), or a company goal that is aligned to the business plan (e.g., we need to increase production this year, thus must complete the project by the third quarter). Problem solving and root cause analysis techniques should always be applied first to determine if a tool is needed and what the tool is needed for.

There are tools for the individuals (a computer), for the team (a CADD tool such as PDS), and tools for the overall organization (a photocopy machine). One should avoid selecting tools for the company to benefit a single individual or a group, unless previously and thoroughly justified.

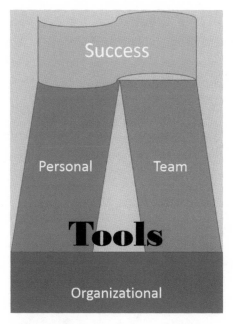

Figure 6 - Tools in Organizations

Things to bear in mind when selecting new tools:

- Tools are created to help us do the job easier, faster, more accurately, with the least effort.

- Tools help us organize things and create the necessary records (documentation).

- Tools are generally task specific.

- Tools are as precise as the available technology would allow them to be. The task dictates the degree of precision required.

- Tools produce the right results, if used as recommended by the manufacturer.

- The data produced by tools is as good as the data we put in them.

- Tools alone cannot solve problems or guarantee quality.

- Tools shall align with the company's mission and vision. A company whose business objective is to be the fastest service provider may not afford to have tools that do not provide the needed speed.

- Tools should be selected on the basis of understanding the need, the tasks required to be performed, and the associated work processes.

- Work processes should be modified to accommodate a new tool, only when benefits surpass the effort and inconveniences of doing it.

- Tools in project management must communicate with each other. Otherwise, we need to create the connections/communication channels to make them useful.

- Adequate use of tools generally requires training of personnel, payment of licenses, and IT support. All of these expenses shall be taken into account in the yearly budgets.

- Obsolete tools shall be promptly revamped or replaced. Change Management is normally required to introduce a new tool into a system.

- There are tools almost for everything; however, only those required should be procured. An excessive number of tools creates confusion, frustration and over-expenditure without necessarily improving performance.

- Tools should be used to check the results of tasks performed and to avoid human error, but should not be used to replace or limit human thinking, innovation, and creativity.

- The effectiveness of the tools and frequency of use should be monitored on a regular basis.

- The selection of tools shall derive from having a clear understanding of the vision, mission, values, standards, systems, and work processes of the company. Tools should not be used to drive the company, since they may drive it in the wrong direction.

A child can probably learn to use a new tool much faster than an adult. This is because they are not affected by previous experiences ("we have always done it that way"), may be more technology-savvy, and is perhaps less afraid to try (because of a natural willingness to step out of the comfort zone).

Training in organizations

Training is an essential part of creating the competency required for your project organization to be sustainable and successful, but the reality is that it's expensive; so many companies end up having to cut on training in order to survive. Whether they realize it or not, in the long run they are hurting their chances of survival.

The basic concepts for achieving the competency levels required to be a top-notch project organization in today's world are:

- Understanding and being ready to communicate with conviction the company's values, mission, standards, and objectives, creating with this a solid base for personnel to perform against.

- Studying and understanding the projects' objectives and requirements.

- Performing risk analysis to understand potential risks and opportunities associated with human resources within the project and the organization, in order to develop training plans that respond to such risks and opportunities.

- Determining the project organization that best suits the project requirements, as part of the project execution planning, and identifying the individuals that will fill out the key positions; preparing roles and responsibilities for each and every position.

- Executing the selection and recruitment necessary to fill out the project organization.

- Performing an organization gap analysis in order to measure how well each and every individual meets the needs of the position, to determine individual strengths, weaknesses, and training requirements.

I have come up with several tools to facilitate the process of measuring the competency gap of your personnel. If you wish to achieve adequate levels of competency within your organization, some analyses are required before attempting to prepare a training plan. Additionally, training of personnel shall be monitored for completeness and effectiveness.

Consider the following:

- Perform a *Project/Customer* gap analysis to measure how well each individual understands the project needs, project complexity, execution strategy, and the customer.

- Perform a *Systems and Tools* gap analysis to measure how well each individual understands the company's systems, tools, and specifications to be utilized in the project.

- Perform a *Work Process* gap analysis, which is used to determine how well each individual understands the work processes they will be involved in, the internal clients and stakeholders, how communication will flow, and how reporting will be performed.

- Determine weaknesses, strengths, and training needs. Draft a training plan for the project organization that addresses all of the above.

- Review and approve the project training plan. Adjust the project budget and schedule, if necessary to match training requirements.

- Implement the training plan.

- Evaluate the status of implementation and effectiveness of the training plan. Make adjustments as required.

The figure below shows the different facets of training of personnel as a work process. Training programs shall exist, be implemented, and measured for effectiveness in the project organization, if wanting to elevate performance.

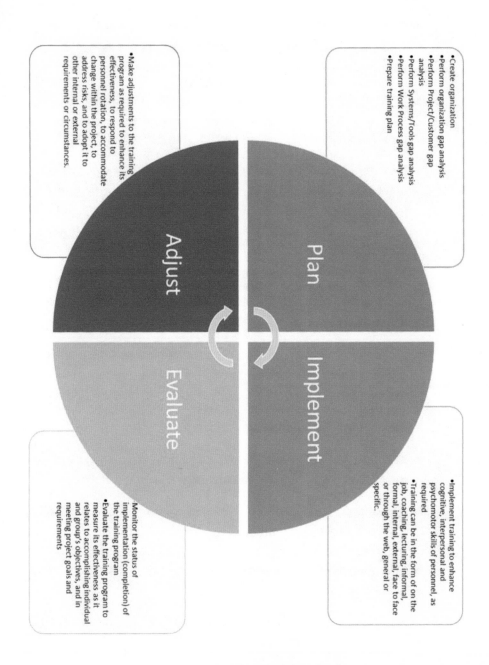

- Create organization
- Perform organization gap analysis
- Perform Project/Customer gap analysis
- Perform Systems/Tools gap analysis
- Perform Work Process gap analysis
- Prepare training plan

- Make adjustments to the training program as required to enhance its effectiveness, to respond to personnel rotation, to accommodate change within the project, to address risks, and to adopt it to other internal or external requirements or circumstances.

Plan

Adjust

Implement

Evaluate

- Implement training to enhance cognitive, interpersonal and psychomotor skills of personnel, as required
- Training can be in the form of on the job, coaching, lecturing, informal, formal, internal, external, face to face or through the web, general or specific.

- Monitor the status of implementation (completion) of the training program
- Evaluate the training program to measure its effectiveness as it relates to accomplishing individual and group's objectives, and in meeting project goals and requirements

Figure 7 - Effective Training Cycle

Roberto Rodriguez Esteves

Roles and responsibilities

Once we have the right amount of people (each of them meeting the competency levels required of their position) and all are utilizing the right tools for the job, what else can help drive up project performance? The answer: Establish, communicate, and practice the roles and responsibilities required of each position. This sounds rather simple, but in reality it is a huge task—one that is seldom well accomplished.

Below is an example that I have put together to explain the importance of understanding roles and responsibilities, and how it goes beyond the individual playing such roles and assuming those responsibilities.

The case of the not-so-useful project controller

Throughout my career, I have had the opportunity to work with very sharp and useful project controllers, and some who were not so. While evaluating those who were successful (and those who were not), I realized there were primarily four kinds of issues related to getting the right support as a project manager from a project controller:

7. Issues associated with roles and responsibilities (What the project controller is supposed to do)

8. Issues tied to their involvement in the different activities required of the position (How the project controller is able to get involved)

9. Issues associated with the methods applied to accomplish the objectives set for that position (What the project controller uses/applies to get the job done)

10. Issues related to how the project manager or leader believed the role of the project controller should be played (How others view the project controller's role being played)

As it relates to the role and responsibilities

The role of a project controller should be that of ensuring the project team (primarily the project manager) has the most current information to make decisions with a clear understanding of their impact on the project schedule and budget. As such, a good project controller should start by making sure the project schedule and budget are realistic, consistent, complete, and properly communicated to all project team members and other key stakeholders.

The second step is to closely monitor the project development in order to compare the actual performance against the plans.

Next, to promptly notify the project team of variations and to draft recovery plans to address such variations.

Finally, and more importantly, to forecast new targets (completion dates and expenditures) for such cases when recovery measures won't be sufficient to hold the slippage.

The ultimate accountability over the budget is on the project manager, yet sometimes project controllers believe they own the project budget, and almost want to keep the expenditure a secret. This could easily create a stressful and conflicting situation, which is not good for neither the project manager nor the project controller.

As it relates to the involvement

The involvement of a project controller is essential for achieving the desired results. Like Quality, if one pretends to control and assure Quality from the outside looking in, the result is that you are seen as a policeman rather than a contributor. Project controlling requires direct and constant involvement with those executing different project activities. It is through building such camaraderie that the project controller may be able to lift the right data at the right time, to allow for decisions to be promptly made to make the necessary corrections and/or re-direct the course, in order to preserve budget and schedule.

Project Control reports are usually generated one or sometimes even two periods after the fact. This is a project killer, since management is not only late but potentially wrong with their decisions, as things would have changed again when making such decisions. With the right involvement, a project controller may increase their ability to produce prompt reports, thus increasing their value to the project team.

As it relates to the methods and tools

Everyone should know and apply the correct methods for project controls, right? So why is it that we have so many methods being applied out there? Why is it that people pretend to control projects without applying earned value? There are common games that go on between owners and contractors; there is a blaming culture whereby it has become easier to hide information until it is too late, or to see if no one would notice. Many reports are created containing half of the information, making it almost impossible for those directing and managing the project to make adequate decisions. Forecasting is probably the worst part. It is not at all uncommon to see forecasts that project a completion based on efficiency of 1.0, in spite of how the project team has underperformed, the budget has been exceeded, and schedule has slipped, with no recovery plan in place.

As it relates to others, particularly the Project Manager

Sadly, there have been times when a project controller clearly understands their role and responsibilities, has had the right involvement, has used the right tools and methodologies, has prepared accurate reports, but has had little support from management. Reports get changed, data is hidden, frustration kicks in, and morale and motivation instantly drop. Who's to blame? Well, these situations are the result of many factors, some of which spread over several organizations, the customers, the contractors and even the vendors.

In my opinion, as long as project controllers don't have clear understanding of their roles and responsibilities, don't have an effective approach and adequate involvement, don't have support from the project organization, and are not obligated to utilize the right methodologies, their effort will be meaningless and the related projects will suffer the consequences.

Everyone's roles and responsibilities need to be openly discussed with those involved in the project, at the early stages of the project. By doing so, more effective organizations will be created while also minimizing the risk of conflict and unproductive work. During these discussions, individuals may present different opinions regarding how their roles should be played. Such discussions shall be resolved on good terms and those involved should agree on how the affected roles will be played.

Not granting someone access to the data and documentation required for the fulfillment of their duties is like not accepting the individual's role as needed for the success of the project team. Leaders, managers, and supervisors shall be attentive to such situations and promptly act to resolve them to assure and retain performance.

Finally, as a project manager, you may decide to question the results presented by a specialist in order to validate that the methodologies, tools, and data used correspond to those that, in your opinion, should have been used. Once those have been validated, and assuming the specialist is both qualified and competent for the task at hand (and that they have used the right methodologies, tools, and sample data) the results should not be questioned, much less changed without the consent of the specialist. This basic principle preserves trust, team collaboration, and leadership.

If for whatever reason (and after discussing the roles and responsibilities of everyone on the team) some duties appear to conflict, intervention may be required to establish the way to proceed (e.g., assign duties to a single individual). Employees stepping on each other's toes is disruptive, ineffective, and sometimes conflictive.

Documenting roles and responsibilities is a healthy step to make sure everyone understands and plays accordingly.

Stakeholders' management

The PMI in their PMBOK – Fifth Edition, Section 13, defines Stakeholders Management as

> "Includes the processes required to identify people, groups, or organizations that could impact or be impacted by the project, to analyze their expectations and impact on the project, and to develop appropriate management strategies for effectively engaging stakeholders in project decisions and execution. It also focuses on continuous communication with stakeholders to understand their needs and expectations, addressing issues as they occur, managing conflicting interests, and fostering appropriate stakeholders engagement in project decisions

and activities. Stakeholder satisfaction should be managed as a key project objective."

A classification of stakeholders would typically be as shown:

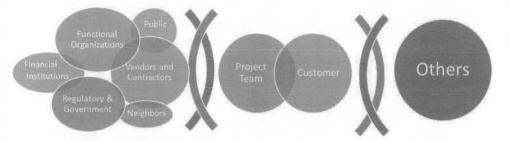

Figure 8 - Different Kinds of Stakeholders

It is precisely the unknown stakeholders who can get your project into trouble. This could be either because your team failed to identify them or because they appear all of a sudden. Let us remember that stakeholder, by definition, is any individual, group, or organization that *can affect, be affected by, or perceive itself to be affected* by a program or project. Sometimes, these unknown stakeholders come from neighborhoods located adjacent to the project site, or they may come from environmentalist groups (such as in the case of Oil & Gas projects) or may come from the competition. The project team must successfully manage stakeholders if expecting to complete the project in time and while complying with project requirements.

I have studied several theories for managing stakeholders. Most of them coincide in measuring two variables to decide the approach you will take toward the stakeholders, namely power and interest (or influence). The theory of power and influence levels to manage stakeholders falls a bit short, in my opinion, for being able to effectively manage them. Why? Well, it assumes that everyone has the same personality, same knowledge, and a good attitude.

Roberto Rodriguez Esteves

My theory for good stakeholder management involves exploring other variables besides power and degree of influence of the individuals, in order to improve your chances of engaging them in a positive manner to aid you in executing your project. A diagram of my stakeholder management approach would look something like this:

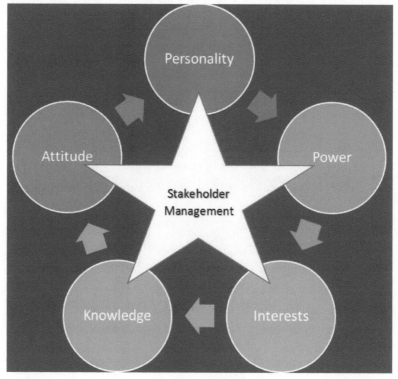

Figure 9 - Variables for Effective Stakeholder Management

Personality

In order to better manage your project stakeholders, study and try to understand their personality, particularly that of the individuals within the internal group of stakeholders. Personalities vary, so we need to vary our approach to individuals in order to enhance the response we will receive in return. Applying the same approach to everyone, regardless of the different personalities, is like tagging everyone with the same label.

Consider the following personality traits, globally known as "the key personality traits":

- *Openness* refers to how inclined someone is to conform to societal or cultural norms, how concretely or abstractly they think about things, and how open or resistant someone is to *change*.

- *Conscientiousness* has to do with a person's degree of organization, level of discipline, and how prone he or she is to taking *risks*.

- *Extraversion* is a personality characteristic that describes things like how social a person is, or how warm and loving they tend to be. In other words, how they *communicate*.

- *Agreeableness* takes into account how kind, dependable, and *cooperative* a person is.

- *Neuroticism* is a personality characteristic that describes how nervous or anxious a person tends to be, as well as the degree of self-confidence and self-contentment he or she possesses. In other words, how they manage *stress*.

Change, risk, communication, cooperation, and stress management. Would you not think that these variables are key components of project execution? How could we afford not to take these variables into account when dealing with the project's stakeholders?

Power

Power is the next component to evaluate when dealing with stakeholders. But first of all, we need to recognize that there are at least seven types of powers:

- Legitimate (official authority)

- Coercive (e.g., bullying at the workplace)

- Expert (based on knowledge and experience)

- Informational (possessing needed or wanted information)

- Reward (linked to who controls raises and bonuses)

- Connection (networking)

- Referent (held by people with charisma, integrity, positive qualities)

We must understand the power each individual in the project organization (and in the organizations of those other stakeholders) have, and draft responses that align with such power levels. Sometimes you will find informal leaders who happen to have lots of power and can either open or close the path for things to come into place, information to flow, or can stand in the way for expediting things.

Interests

Some theories discuss the interests different stakeholders have on the project as the only element of this variable. I think it goes beyond this. Consider, for example, that you have a project organization with mixed interests, where you find stakeholders with interest in:

- *Their career/themselves:* Only things that directly or indirectly affect their career and progress motivate individuals with this category of interest.

- *Being the leader:* There are individuals who are only interested in participating if they can lead; otherwise they are not interested. They will usually assume a somewhat indifferent and retracted position in the team when not leading.

- *Money:* Occasionally we find individuals who are not motivated at all by the project or being part of the team. They are there just for the money. Sometimes it is about individuals who are reaching retirement but cannot afford to quit just yet; at other times it is about people with little motivation, no desire for growth, or who are unhappy about their role but unable or unwilling to make a change for the better.

- *Reporting/receiving reports:* These are individuals who generally like to see official reports of some form or another so they can understand what is going on, critique the results, or make decisions. Unfortunately for the project, excessive reporting may mean less work on productive tasks which ultimately get further behind. On the other hand, some may regard this issue as lack of trust from the party requesting a formal report for everything, which may affect relationships in the long run. Promptly-generated, concise, and properly-timed reporting is most effective.

- *Relationships/team:* There are those who are genuinely interested in building relationships and socializing while the project gets implemented. This is generally a good interest to have in the project team, as it cuts the ice, combats stress, and foments collaboration among peers. Caution shall be exercised when excessive socializing is practiced, potentially leading to people spending more time talking about personal matters than producing results for the project.

- *Safety and environment:* This is a great interest to have. Those who care about safety and environment will likely perform their duties while preserving these values. They will raise a flag when something appears to be out of order, may be unsafe, or cause an incident. Coaching and close supervision may be required when working with individuals who are generally risk takers, messy, or careless about the impact their actions may have on the environment.

- *Quality of work:* These are the individuals who will be on the watch for deliverables and services to be of the right quality before hitting the door. They will raise questions when data, time or budget does not match what is needed to produce sound and good quality deliverables and services. Excessive reiterations of deliverables may be a sign of wanting to gold plate it, or of seeking perfection. Intervention may be required in such cases to take the team back to what is required by the project, and raise consciousness of the project budget and schedule limitations.

- *Learning/knowledge:* Some just want to learn. They learn on each project as if they were a sponge. The moment that no learning is experienced, they tend to feel that the use of their time is not effective, which may lead to seeking other opportunities where they can continue to learn. As supervisors, when we spot these individuals, we need to try to get them involved in challenging activities, pushing them into areas where learning will be more probable. Ultimately, we need to work on their patience and place importance back on achieving the goals of the project, showing them that it is their path toward moving into more interesting positions where learning new things will be possible.

- *Project success:* Ideally, everyone should be interested in achieving project success, and this is generally the case. What is key is where they place project success on their list of priorities. Most individuals will have some personal objective or another that weighs more than the collective project success. Still, no one likes to be associated to failing projects, so it's not unusual to see people pitching in to get it done, sometimes sacrificing one or more of their other more personal objectives. Project managers that are able to make the project success their team's success will generally have greater chances of completing the project as per requirements.

Can you afford to have the same approach to each and every individual in your project organization? How much time as a project manager do you invest in finding out the different interests of the people in your project team?

Knowledge

Knowledge is defined as facts, information, and skills acquired through experience or education; it is also the theoretical or practical understanding of a subject. When I refer to understanding knowledge of stakeholders in your project, I mean to inquire about and validate the following:

- *Knowledge of the task—work process:* People come from different places and have different experiences and approaches regarding how to perform certain tasks or execute certain work processes. We need to create affinity amongst stakeholders as to how the work will be executed while resolving potential conflicts that will emerge from my way of doing versus yours.

- *Knowledge and experience in project execution:* Project teams are composed of resources of different ages and experience levels. Beyond the knowledge of the tasks and work processes lies the knowledge in project execution. How many projects has each stakeholder executed in the past? What was the size and complexity of the project? What role did they play? Were the strategies effectively implemented?

- *Knowledge and experience in project management:* Having executed projects in the past does not necessarily prepare you for assuming a leading role within a project. Stakeholders in leading positions who do not have the necessary knowledge and experience in those roles may pose a risk to the project. Since sometimes this is out of our control, we must find ways of closing the gap and seeking alignment on things that matter and affect the project's outcome.

- *Previous good or bad experiences:* People who have worked on a series of failed projects may not have learned the necessary elements for achieving success. Their performance may be partially affected by such limitations, which at times only exists in their minds (perceived but not real).

- *Perceptions—pretending or perceived as knowledgeable:* This refers to people who pretend to be knowledgeable about a subject, but really aren't. It normally takes some time for anyone to notice that they lack the necessary knowledge to perform one task or another. On the contrary, sometimes people are perceived as expert in their discipline, which may lead to others constantly interrupting their work to seek advice. Either case may be disruptive and/or cause delays in the project.

- *Trust levels—sharing of knowledge:* Some people are very jealous of the knowledge they possess and do not want to share it with others. Knowledge sharing could at times be confused with *critical-for-the-project* information sharing. Intervention is required when information does not seem to flow out of an individual's office, which can occur when they consider it to be *their* knowledge and are unwilling to share.

- *Influence of cultural and language barriers:* Language and cultural barriers are sometimes the most difficult to overcome—in part because we don't necessarily understand them. People who come from different parts of the world have learned things in slightly different ways. When bringing them together, some inefficiencies may result.

Dealing with knowledge in different forms as explained above is essential for managing stakeholders.

Attitude

Attitude is perhaps the most difficult variable to evaluate as it can change constantly. Attitude is defined as a feeling or way of thinking that affects a person's behavior.

Some signs of attitude are not even expressed with words, but rather through corporal language. Some people may be telling you something when they mean something else. Some signs of attitude are:

- Friendly and helpful

- Threatening and hostile

- Negative

- Cool, cocky, defiant, arrogant

- Ignoring, not paying attention

- Conflictive

- Selfish

- In despair or affected

- Caring and responsive

Attitude may be affected by circumstances inside or outside of the project environment, such as a family or personal crisis, missing a promotion, previously-acquired commitments, health issues, etc.

Part of being a good leader or a good team player is the ability to identify when a partner or subordinate is affected by circumstances and may not necessarily have the best attitude. Those are moments when encouragement and support may pay more dividends than judgment and neglect.

Stakeholder management should be practiced by all rather than just by the project manager. The opportunity is there to manage stakeholders for each work process. If individuals in the project organization get accustomed to practicing stakeholder management, the probability of increasing their satisfaction is materialized.

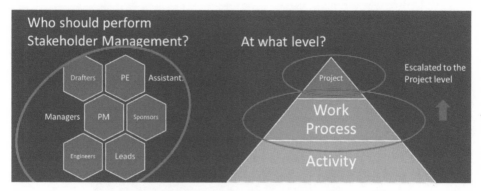

Figure 10 - Effective Stakeholder Management

Stakeholder management is an important component of successful project execution. It requires discipline and attention to details. The following are recommended steps for effective stakeholder management:

- Identify who your stakeholders are.

- Study the contractual requirements and stated expectations (this could be the first step as well).

- Perform interviews with a predetermined checklist of things to ask. Try to identify where they are strong and where there might be some flexibility. Also, try to identify leadership levels and recognize who is in charge of making decisions or influencing them. Some questions should measure the maturity and comprehension level each stakeholder has over project execution and management. Mature and experienced people are more conscious of the impact their unstated needs and expectations may have in the execution of the project, and of your ability to cope with them for fulfillment.

- State your needs and expectations to them as well, particularly to those stakeholders who you will require assistance, input, or collaboration from. At the end of the session, read back to them what you have stated and, if possible, ask them to provide acknowledgement.

- Perform an internal evaluation with your project team to discuss the stakeholder's needs and expectations, the risks of not meeting such needs and expectations, and verbal versus written requirements and/or expectations.

- Review your project strategic and execution plans and identify any gaps or areas of attention where your plans may not be addressing the stakeholder's needs and expectations (even if such needs and expectations are not written in the contractual documents but have been clearly expressed). Make adjustments to the plans as required.

- Hold regular meetings with key stakeholders to assess project performance against known needs and expectations. Seek feedback, record it, and monitor it against previously-stated needs and expectations. If noticing that they have considerably changed, initiate Change Management.

- Based on such feedback, create action plans for those areas where needs or expectations may be compromised. Make sure that root causes are identified in support of creating the most effective action plans. If at all possible, each area where needs or expectations are compromised should be linked to related work processes. It is the fixing or adjusting of such work processes that may lead to the fastest and most effective fulfillment of unmet needs and expectations.

- Stay positive but firm; elevate issues when conflict appears to be inevitable and/or issues become unmanageable.

Roberto Rodriguez Esteves

Documenting stakeholder management may be rather trouble-some and ineffective. I have put together a chart that will assist you in documenting the different steps. At least four templates are needed to follow this approach for documenting stake-holder management:

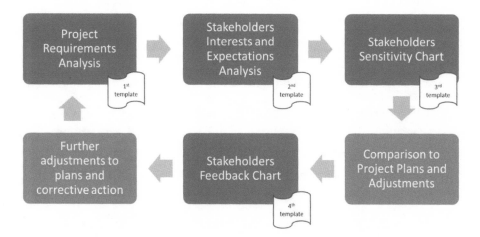

Figure 11 - Documenting Stakeholder Management

The *Project Requirements Analysis* is done by the project team based on contractual information shared by the project owner, before interviews with the different stakeholders are conducted. The idea is to seek common understanding amongst team members of the project requirements, as presented by the project owner in the contractual documentation (including referenced specifications, standards, policies, and procedures).

The *Stakeholders Interests and Expectations Analysis* is done through interviews and other means of communication to pre-cisely lift the necessary data that clearly describes the project requirements and expectations as seen by the stakeholders. It is the most common step executed by project organizations to manage stakeholders.

The *Stakeholders Sensitivity Analysis*—trying to understand what stakeholders are sensitive to the most. Usually you will find stakeholders who are mostly concerned with not exceeding the budget; others want it done by a certain date, others are more concerned with achieving the function for which it is being designed, and a few others are mostly concerned with safety. Whether it is cost, quality, time, safety, user-friendly, while following procedures, or whatever their sensitivity area is, finding out ahead of engaging in the execution of the project sets the project team in a better position to satisfy the expectations of their stakeholders. Conflicting priorities will likely exist, but they are better managed when known upfront.

The *Stakeholders Feedback Analysis* gathers their feedback on how the project team in doing with respect to meeting project requirements, as well as stakeholders needs and expectations. Adjustments to the plans or to the approach taken by the project team normally emerge of such feedback.

Things to remember about Stakeholder Management:

- Performed by all

- Done regularly and systematically

- Carried out at the work process level and then escalated to the project level

- Based on sharing, understanding and trying to meet expectations from both sides

- While taking into account personality, power, interests, knowledge, and attitude

- It should be documented

- Measured by performance and results through collecting feedback from those affected by and/or involved in the project

Team Performance

You have done all you can to put together a qualified team within your project organization, and now should invest some time into creating the programs for measuring performance. Only by lifting this data can you continuously improve the management and quality of human resources.

As seen in Table 2 below, each individual participating in any of the project execution phases would be measured against established parameters for decision making, leadership and direction, problem-solving abilities, technical knowledge, skills, and abilities, project management knowledge, skills, and abilities, and administrative and computer skills.

This approach to measuring human resources performance, rather than just measuring the accomplishment of objectives, directs the attention to key areas that more directly affect project execution, but are seldom evaluated.

The accomplishment of goals in team environments is usually the result of everyone doing what they are supposed to do, safely, on time, with quality, and within the assigned budget. If instead people focus solely on accomplishing objectives at any cost, they may succeed, but other issues such as conflict, unsatisfied stakeholders, bias decisions, missing or hidden information, or even back-stabbing may occur. Thus, the suggestion to take a more comprehensive approach toward measuring team performance.

I have assembled a Work Breakdown Structure (WBS) that shows the "Team Performance" work process broken down to four levels. The variables described in Level 3 with K.P.I's as shown in Level 4, are applicable to each and every business / project phase, as described in Level 2 of the WBS.:

Level 1	Team Performance				
Level 2	Business Identification	Selection Phase	Project Execution Phase		During Operations
Level 3	Decision Making	Leadership and Direction	Problem Solving	Technical Performance	Project Management & Administrative Performance
Level 4	• Timely • Well informed • With the involvement of those affected • Assertive • Followed up	• Approachable • Clear direction • Good communication • Walks the talk • Leads for all and with all • Supportive • Friendly • Consistent • Good planning	• Problem well defined • Root Cause(s) determined • Action Plan prepared and carried out • Followed up properly • Continuous Improvement achieved • Timely	• Qualified • Updated with latest technologies and best practices • Properly sequenced • High safety and quality oriented • Team approach • Effective problem solving	• Well Planned • Transparent • Well documented • Win-Win approach • Based on clear objectives • Effective Communication • Risk conscious • Client Management • Balanced • Team approach • Effective problem solving

Table 2 - Team Performance Table

Roberto Rodriguez Esteves

People working in healthy organizations where respect, collaboration, trust, and empowerment exist produce optimum results.

We should invest more time walking the floors, talking to people in person, listening to them, finding ways to help them out; this creates working environments that produce optimum results.

Management of human beings starts with your ability to manage yourself, your desire to assist and help others, and your ability to create trust and followers. Some tips to help you get there are the following:

- Try to balance your life (spirit, family, health, community, work).

- Practice effective time management (prioritize, plan).

- Acknowledge that problem solving is an essential part of your job and your life.

- Know that you cannot solve a problem or make assertive decisions when uninformed. Focus your attention to early problem identification and data collection.

- Make sure root causes are properly identified and analyzed.

- Prepare a response plan that most directly acts on root causes, preferably with your team.

- Seek corroboration, endorsement, and buy-in from involved people of the action plan—then implement it!

- Follow up on actions taken until proven effective; repeat analysis as needed until issue or problem is totally resolved. Record additional lessons.

Chapter Five: Coping with Change

I'd like to start this chapter on change by providing you with some famous quotes about change, made by truly inspiring people:

> Change is the law of life. And those who look only to the past or present are certain to miss the future.
> —*John F. Kennedy*

> You must be the change you wish to see in the world.
> —*Mahatma Gandhi*

> Progress is impossible without change, and those who cannot change their minds cannot change anything.
> — *George Bernard Shaw*

> The first step toward change is awareness. The second step is acceptance.
> —*Nathaniel Branden*

> Since we cannot change reality, let us change the eyes which see reality.
> —*Nikos Kazantzakis*

> For the past thirty-three years, I have looked in the mirror every morning and asked myself, 'If

today were the last day of my life, would I want to do what I am about to do today?' And whenever the answer has been 'No' for too many days in a row, I know I need to change something.
—*Steve Jobs*

Change is unavoidable and must be planned for and managed.

The mere concept of change has many interpretations. Some may not see changes happening in front of them, because they only look for change of the most evident kind: scope change. However, there are many kinds of changes that require attention, such as changes in specifications, regulations, laws, project location or conditions, personnel, leadership, objectives, priorities, tools, systems, infrastructure, methods, testing procedures, motivation, mood and attitude, communications, weather, productivity, availability of equipment, suppliers, among others.

The list is almost endless!

Can one person in the project team be sufficient for managing the entire gamut of changes? Likely not. Some people believe that by adding a change manager to the project team, change will take care of itself. Nonsense! That is the same as pretending to avoid safety incidents by adding a safety officer, or thinking that quality standards will be met by having a quality manager assigned to the project. These professionals are there to guide the team on the how and what is required to achieve a change, safety, and quality culture in a project organization. They should not be there to maintain logs and issue tickets to people who don't follow the rules and/or assume the wrong behaviors.

The problem is that some managers believe such measures are effective. They do not want to be accountable, so the first and most obvious thing to do is to assign such accountability on somebody else. Unfortunately, they fail to realize that if the person now holding accountability does not also have the authority, control, and power to do what is required to revert the poor behaviors and change the culture, they will hit their head against the wall and fail at the assigned duties.

Most of us grew up watching Hollywood movies—good old western movies, spy movies, or good cop-bad guy movies. The one thing in common is that there is always a hero and a villain. Sometimes, we seem to take what we have learned while watching these movies into the workplace. We love to see cops and bad guys at the workplace, and so many assign Quality Managers as cops and employees not following the rules of engagement as bad guys. The same is expected for managing change, risk, and safety, to name a few. Why do we love taking the responsibility out of everyone's hands and placing it in the hands of one single person?

Don't we realize that by doing so, we are actually creating mediocre professionals who prefer to execute the work as they wish until they are otherwise caught, rather than doing it right from the beginning? Who is more qualified to identify change, risk, quality, and safety issues with what is being done than the employee directly involved in it?

Change is natural, and as such, everyone—absolutely everyone—shall be part of this process. Work processes need to be there to teach project team members how to identify change, what constitutes a change, how to process a change, when not to work on a change, how to implement change effectively, etc. When we do this, and make it part of everyone's regular duties, we move toward establishing a "Change Culture". The second step is to safely implement change.

Management of change, MOC, or safe implementation of change is regarded by many as something done for safety. I regard it as the necessary steps to evaluate risks and opportunities associated to the implementation of a change, and then drafting the necessary response to assure such change is implemented safely, but also with quality and while preserving performance.

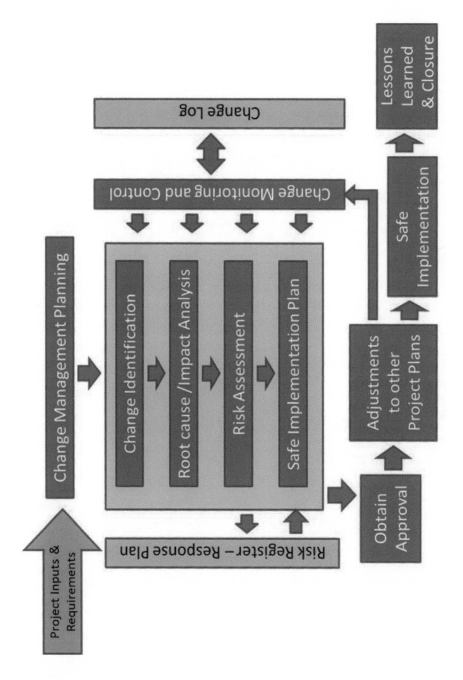

Figure 12 - Change Management Process Workflow

Safe implementation in a broader sense, simply says, "Do it right, while taking the time to assess the potential impact of change beyond its immediate and most evident effect." Failing to do this can increase the impact of the change.

What is the greatest challenge associated to safe implementation of change beyond having to learn how to apply risk and quality management to change? Well, time! Yes, everyone wants change to be implemented right away—sometimes even before it is approved—leaving little chance for anyone trying to do it right to take the time to perform a brief risk analysis, and to quantify a more realistic impact of the change being considered for implementation.

A holistic and systemic approach to change implies getting people used to performing risk and impact analysis as a natural step when evaluating it. Without doubt, getting everyone used to managing change with this perspective is not easily achieved.

It wasn't until people decided to take safety seriously that we started to see improvement in the implementation of programs to create and establish "safety culture" in project organizations. It took many injuries and the loss of many lives for governments to act and push toward elevating safety performance throughout most industries. One can still find construction sites with poor safety culture, and they usually carry a high incident rate as well. I have seen companies try to revert their high incident rates by applying ineffective measures such as adding more safety officers, or even worse, taking disciplinary action against employees caught violating the safety rules and policies. They fail to modify the behavior because they do not target the root cause of the problem.

Safety culture at a construction site won't likely be established until people (everyone, including employees, vendors, contractors, visitors) decide to practice safe behavior by choice. In order for people to naturally adopt a safe behavior and to show a collaborative approach toward the safety of everyone at site, they must first understand and value safety. Through coaching, training, awareness, support, incentive programs, and lots of modeling from management and supervisory staff, they will adopt the right behavior.

One of the most beautiful things to observe at a construction site is when you see everyone truly committed to safety. Tools are checked regularly and tagged, workers wear protective equipment at all times, signage is up, garbage and rubbish is put away, dust is controlled, safety talks and hazards analysis are performed on a daily basis with the crews that will execute the related tasks, safety inspections are regularly done, all incidents and near misses are reported, and when so required, investigated, everyone works by approved permits, heavy equipment is inspected regularly, lifts are done with adequate load-trajectory evaluation, everyone is responsible for safety, accountability is placed on the project manager, construction manager, and all line supervisors rather than on the safety officer, and so on.

What do you think is the effect of establishing a safety culture at a construction site as it relates to productivity?

> "A workforce that is dedicated to the habit of excellence in safety is dedicated to performing their jobs the right way. When an organization makes safety their core value, greater productivity will follow."
> —*Joe Stevens, Safety Consultant,*
> *expert in Safety Culture, and founder*
> *of Bridge Safety Consultants.*

In summary, when a company decides to establish a work process and does it well, employees generally respond in a positive manner. Let us now apply the same concepts and principles of "safety management" into "change management". The following could be said:

- In order to modify the behaviors of people toward change, we need to first make change a normal and to some extent expected phenomenon. *In similar fashion, safety should be understood as a value, and everyone shall be committed to safety.*

- We must remove fear of dealing with change. People need to feel comfortable identifying change. Managers need to get used to managing it, always seeking adequate justification before approving it. *Likewise, people must get used to performing hazards analysis and obtaining a work permit prior to starting activities, and must be able to stop work if a safety concern arises without fear that disciplinary actions might be taken upon them for reporting the safety concern or stopping work.*

- Risks of implementation and potential impact on other variables (people, training, safety, quality, etc.) shall be assessed prior to approving changes. *Similarly, safety hazards and other risks are assessed before entering a construction site.*

- Estimating the impact of change has to account for the change itself and all known actions (responses) required to safely implement the change. *This is like evaluating the impact of an incident. It not only covers the assessment of the personal injuries that it caused, but other factors such as physical damage to equipment and materials, loss of continuity and production, low morale of personnel leading to low productivity, claims and law suits, etc.*

- No one should work on changes which have not been properly evaluated and given approval. *In the same way, no one should enter an excavation still under construction, climb on a scaffold still being assembled, or use a tool or equipment for which they have not been trained on.*

- Employees should be recognized when coming up with creative ideas to reduce the impact of change, which at times may represent avoiding the change entirely. *This is like recognizing employees that report near misses (potential hazards) before the occurrence of a safety incident.*

- Do not create bureaucratic approval processes. Make it simple and practical so everyone is inclined to identify change and manage it, rather than hiding it, or working on it as if it were part of the original scope and conditions. *Likewise, you should make it simple and practical, so people report incidents at the work place.*

As you can see, we can take a mature work process and use it as an example to improve other work processes, particularly those work processes based on the same sort of principles, and which require people to adopt the right behaviors and attitude.

Chapter Six: If Risks Weren't There, Life Would Be Boring

Risk Management: the most unmanaged area of the business!

Risks come in different forms and shapes, from big to small, from hard to soft, from technical to non-technical, from immediate to distant.

Why is it so difficult to have a culture of "risk awareness" in our project organizations?

Perhaps because risks refer to events of the future. Some of us are good at predicting the future, but others feel uncomfortable with its uncertainties.

Risk Management requires systemic analysis! which is described as:

> A way of thinking. It is a way of putting together the pieces of information we have to create an understanding of the whole. Learning to see from a systemic analysis approach requires that we be willing to move ideas and pieces of information around in our mind and in our understanding. What seem to be isolated events are rarely that. Events have causes and effects. As we examine

the information about the events, we arrange and rearrange the ideas that the information generates. Usually, patterns become visible. These patterns enable us to see the systems that are involved in the events.[1]

When Risk Management is not approached through systemic analysis, risks sessions tend to be too general and superficial, people measure the probability and consequences of risks very subjectively. Underestimation of probability and consequences of risks is a major cause of projects failing, if and when hit by such risks. Thus the importance of preparing risks session way in advance, having the most suitable and experienced people in the room, following a sound methodology, and having the right leadership and guidance so that proper evaluation is achieved for all risks and opportunities that are identified.

Does Risk Management take time and effort? Yes! And how much time and effort do we usually have for Risk Management? Well, some project managers would argue, "Why spend time and resources on what could happen in the future? We don't know if it is really going to happen." Not very clever!, I would say.

Poor planning is potentially the most destructive ally of poor risk management; the two combined can easily lead to trouble in project management. Project teams in these situations soon find themselves putting out fires and running around to make things happen, always in a reactive mode.

This is nothing more than our inability to plan and work on what is important yet not urgent (quadrant 2). Stephen Covey called it "beginning with the end in mind". Projects with little time and effort on planning tend to be projects that react to risks rather than having a plan to either treat or prevent them from occurring.

---

1 Taken from CREA at http://crea.org/systemic-analysis/systemic-analysis/

Another constraint to proper risk management is the misunderstanding of what contingency is for and how it is used in project management. Most people tend to place contingency around known issues that could be planned for, or that they know will occur, rather than placing it around the unknowns (risks). When evaluating contingency as it is expended in projects, you will notice that in the majority of cases, it is expended too soon—sometimes on risks that strike the project, but which were not assessed; thus no mitigation took place; more often expended to manage changes of scope.

The third aspect is in our nature. Some project teams and project managers assume the hero approach to project management. "Yes, NOTHING can stop us now!" We know all too well that such approach in life does not get us far, so why would we expect different results while executing projects?

The inability to plan, inadequate use of contingency, and an overly-risky attitude create the perfect excuse for project managers and their teams to perform poor risk management, or to skip it altogether. The consequences, as discussed in chapter two, could easily drive the project to failure.

I don't want to bore you with too much detail on the process of risk management; there is plenty of information that can be found on the web and other sources like the PMBOK. But generally speaking, the risk management work process should cover planning, identification, analysis, response, and follow-up. It should be a documented process. Please refer to the flowchart shown below for more details.

Perhaps the most important risks to manage are those associated to health, safety, and environmental protection and preservation. They tend to populate the Risk Registers fast, but sometimes do not receive the attention that they deserve.

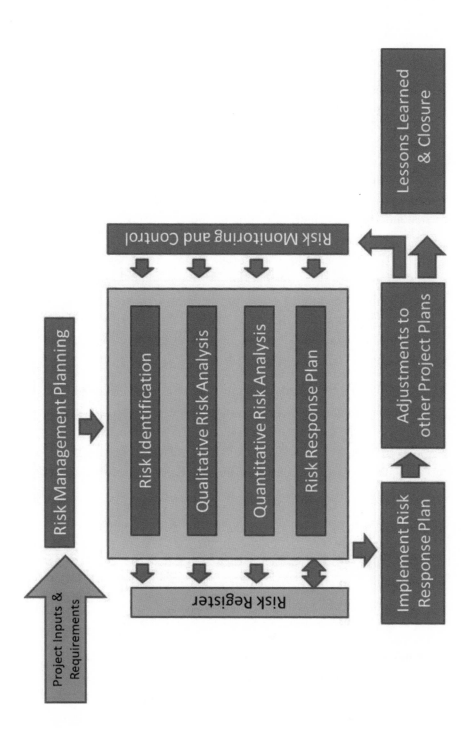

Figure 13 - Risk Management Process Workflow

Another group of risks that seem to be affecting projects is the so-called Non-Technical Risk group. It is defined as all risks and opportunities that emerge from interactions with regulatory, public, socio-economic, governmental, non-governmental, and environmental organizations for the management of related aspects of a project's operations.

According to an article recently published by Valiant & Company Ltd, out of the UK, "Companies in energy and mining are facing real and growing costs from non-technical risks driven by communities, governments, non-government organizations and media—both social and traditional." They claim that according to their own studies, international oil companies' projects now take double the time to come online compared with a decade ago, causing significant increase in costs. In their opinion, non-technical risks account for nearly half the total risks, with stakeholder-related risks the largest category.

Another source I consulted on this subject was the Society of Petroleum Engineers —SPE International and the Australian Petroleum Production and Exploration Association Ltd. They claim that based on data collected over the years, non-technical risks can account for up to 70 – 75% of cost and schedule failures in projects.

These reports seem to validate the importance of looking at the overall project execution failure problem as a whole, where risk, change, quality, decisions, communications, and stakeholder management integrate to become a robust solution.

Risk Management is often pushed aside and ignored on the pretext of being time-consuming and a bunch of witchcraft. Project owners at times do not want to allocate funds on things that no one knows for sure will actually happen. This is to some extent fair, but short-minded and rather optimistic. Our best tool to overcome this issue is to establish the necessary work processes for managing risk while engaging risk experts to validate that such work processes are understood and practiced, draft and review the procedures, and intervene when needed to provide advice.

Chapter Seven: Quality as an Intrinsic Variable, Naturally Achieved

Quality is in everything you do. Doing everything with quality is not a given, though. It comes through a continuous learning process that accepts failure as a significant contributor, aided by the ability to transform substandard work processes into effective ones.

In today's competitive world, service companies must excel at all aspects of the work. Hourly rates alone are no longer sufficient for winning jobs. One area of the business that is usually sacrificed (when budgets are short or overrun and schedules are tight) is quality. Some statements that could help in explaining what happens with quality in projects are:

- Traditionally, cost and schedule take priority over quality.

- Poor decisions or lack of attention to the fulfillment of work process requirements will cause quality to drop.

- Customers are becoming more stringent, reducing execution schedules to the bare minimum.

- Service companies are having to face lower profit margins as a result of poor performance, rework, inconsistencies and system failures.

- Personnel turnover causes loss of continuity, more training of personnel, and inefficiencies, among other consequences that aggravate the situation.

- Placing the focus around the following of procedures, while failing to learn the work processes in the constantly-changing environment of project execution, leads to trouble.

- A Quality Culture is hardly established.

- Quality is usually taken as reacting to things that go wrong or deliverables that are defective or not meeting requirements. Organizations that rely on reactive measures rather than proactive ones for quality are destined to fail.

When all competitors are able to produce results with similar hours and costs (examples: engineering firms, fabricators, etc.), the advantage becomes doing the work at higher quality levels with less rework. Some organizations recognize this, so they invest in creating a Quality Management System (mostly made of procedures), and then certify the system to ISO 9001. Despite obtaining the certification from a qualified agency, they may still not have success at executing projects, either because the system is not effective, or because personnel do not follow the system. I spent years trying to upgrade a Quality Management System for an engineering firm only to realize that project managers chose not to follow the system. Upon performing audits and bringing legitimate findings to management, they showed openness and gratitude for a job well done, but little action was taken to revert the situation, force managers to use the system, and address the findings until closure (including lessons to be learned). After several months, and while the organization executed several other projects, additional audits were performed resulting in the same types of issues with unfortunate recurring consequences.

Quality is not a complex subject in itself. People tend to make it something difficult to achieve, primarily because of their lack of commitment to producing something as per standards and requirements—that is, their inability to treat Quality as a value not to be sacrificed at any cost.

One thing is for sure: if we are to treat Quality as a value, we must learn the basics around quality management, control, and assurance. This means sharing understanding within the project organization on the following: quality concepts, problem solving, learning lessons, continuous improvement, and performance indicators. The next sections are dedicated to expanding on these subjects.

Quality Concepts

Quality management is the process for ensuring that all project activities necessary to design, plan, and implement a project are effective and efficient with respect to the purpose of the objective and its performance.

Project quality management is not a separate, independent process that occurs at the end of an activity to measure the level of quality of the output.

Quality and grade are not the same; grade are characteristics of a material or service such as additional features. A product may be of good quality (no defects) and be of low grade (few or no extra features).

Quality management is a continuous process that starts and ends with the project. It is more about preventing and avoiding than measuring and fixing poor quality outputs. It is part of every project management process, from the moment the project initiates to the final steps in the project closure phase.

Quality Management focuses on improving customer satisfaction through the continuous and incremental improvement of work processes, which translates in better products and services, and ultimately more value for their money:

- Quality is a way of thinking.

- Quality is in everything that we do.

- Quality should be both proactive and planned for.

- Quality should be treated as a corporate value, like safety. It has to be part of the company's corporate culture

- Quality improvement shall be both planned and properly budgeted for.

Quality Management Planning includes not only developing a quality plan, but ensuring project team personnel, contractors, vendors, suppliers, etc. have the necessary information, tools, materials, specifications, systems, and so on to deliver quality of products and services that fully meet the project requirements.

A workflow of the Quality Management work processes is shown below:

The Quality Management System is designed to prevent undesired events from occurring. However, if and when such events do occur, personnel must act to determine why they happened and how to fix what caused them so they will not recur.

- The organization must have the capability and authority to make improvements to the system.

- Events are generally the consequence of a failure in the system.

- Analysis must be systematic and thorough, preferably at the work process level—linking the problem to the closest work process to determine if it was faulty, incomplete, inadequately performed, poorly documented, not normed, etc.

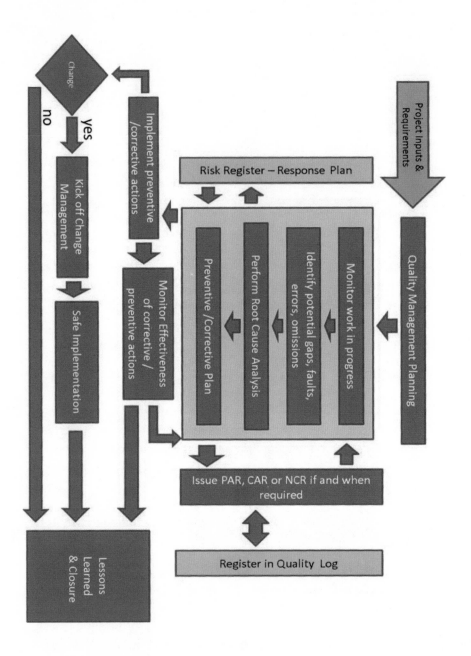

Figure 14 - Quality Management Process Workflow

Roberto Rodriguez Esteves

- Root cause analysis shall be performed while utilizing a proven and suited methodology. *Suited* means that the methodology should be suited to the type and complexity of the issue at hand.

- Causes shall be prioritized from most influential on the undesired event, problem, or issue to the least influential, while using the PARETO Analysis or alike.

- Action plans shall be prepared to address at least the 20% of the root causes of the undesired event, issue, or problem that appear to be responsible for the undesired event, issue, or problem 80% of the time.

- Actions shall be implemented, monitored, and measured for effectiveness. If the undesired result, issue, or problem reoccurs, then further analysis and subsequent application of additional corrective actions may be required.

- Lessons shall be raised while making sure they are truly learned throughout the organization (implemented within the system).

Problem Solving

Problem solving is defined as using generic and *ad hoc* methods to resolve problems. When executing projects, many types of problems could evolve. Whether technical or non-technical, procedural or system-related, poor scope definition or people-related problems, the project team must become good at resolving them. Different steps for effective problem solving, and typical action taken, are described below.

Six steps to successful problem solving:

- *Identify the problem*—Assertively describe what is happening that requires resolution/action.

- *Collect data*—Fact-find while involving people.

- *Analyze*—Determine root causes and possible responses.

- *Make recommendations, seek endorsement, and act*—Draft a response action plan and have it corroborated, endorsed, and implemented.

- *Follow-up*—Validate effectiveness of actions in resolving the problem. Repeat above steps if problem does not seem to be properly addressed with taken action plan.

- *Closure*—Bring it to closure while recording all learning for future reference

There are different responses we can adopt to resolve problems. The chart below shows the effectiveness of each:

It is upon the project team to choose the response that best suits the problem at hand. The effectiveness of the solution is linked to the response given, where "problem solving" appears to be the effective response for most of the cases.

Method	Advantages	Disadvantages	Effectiveness
Ignore	Easy, quick, least involvement	Problem will grow	Low
Transfer	Easy, quick, some involvement	Person receiving the problem may not effectively resolve it	Low- Medium
Act by Authority	Fast, done as per one's wish, enhances ego and self respect	May create false impression on success, affects people, subject to own perceptions, least appreciated by others	Low
Mediate	Decision is more informed, utilizes people's skills	One may be seen as impartial, loss of trust, affects one side	Medium
Problem Solve	Full use of people's skills, more effective and just to involved parties, least susceptible to reoccurrence. Strengthens team	Takes time, effort, concentration, patience and will. Requires skills	High

Table 3 - Problem Solving Techniques

Why is it that my kite won't fly?

Learning Lessons

The principle behind lessons is to be able to process them within the system until they are truly learned. This implies a series of steps shall take place prior to achieving this valuable milestone. Capturing lessons and not processing them, or only partially acting on them, provides no learning; thus recurrence of issues shall be expected.

The key elements of gathering and learning lessons are:

- Obtaining valuable input from personnel on positive and negative learning experiences while on a project.

- Obtaining feedback from everyone involved and at as many levels within the project organization as possible. This will lead to more balanced and precise lessons.

- Gathering and recording data on a frequent basis (daily if possible) while associating the lessons to the most affected by work process.

- Exercising care to avoid personalizing the issues while maintaining focus on achieving system improvement.

- Compiling all lessons in a "Project Lessons" database

- Performing Root Cause Analysis to determine causal factors, and preparing action plans to realize the desired system improvement.

- Assuring adequate implementation of the action plans, with training of personnel (when so required).

- Following up to check on the effectiveness of the action plans (response) recently implemented, and drafting new plans when required to assure lessons are truly learned and associated incidents do not recur.

- Document learning and seek continuous improvement thereafter.

Lessons shall lead to improving the system today in order to better execute projects in the future. To better implement lessons, it is suggested to create a database. I have seen many databases that do not really help implementation, either because they are too extensive, or impractical, or are not accompanied by a thorough analysis of the causes that originally led to the issue or incident captured.

The database shall be organized in such a way that information is systematically stored; the data can be segregated as required by the user, tracking to closure if possible; most importantly, it can be used to improve the system today (not used to store information without action).

A quality assurance process is required to keep the database current, organized, logical and concise.

The Root Cause Analysis (RCA) is the most important step in processing lessons. Not performing this crucial step or doing it poorly will lead to not acting on the true causes, thus not learning the lesson. The methodology used can vary from three simple "whys" to a more complex TapRooT® analysis. The important thing is to prepare and retain a record of the analysis made in support of your action plans. Always try to identify the work process that failed as part of your analysis. Process improvement is the ultimate goal. If actions taken do not seem effective, a more in-depth RCA may be required

Close a lesson only once it has become evident that the lesson has been truly learned and the system has been upgraded.

There are many benefits in capturing, processing, and learning lessons. Some of the more evident ones that come to mind are:

- Higher business performance

- Greater commitment from our personnel to do things better the next time around

- Less rework and higher productivity

- Improved communication

- Increased ownership by our personnel of their work processes and procedures

- More robust system

- Higher client satisfaction

- More successful project execution

- Higher profit margins, which leads to happier shareholders and company growth

- Safer, healthier, and more environmentally-protected projects

I have now given you the ABCs of learning lessons—so how come this appears to be such a difficult task to accomplish in project organizations? Through internal and external audits where I was involved either as a customer or as an auditor, one thing seemed to be common in organizations that fail to record, analyze, and learn lessons: it is seen as a time-consuming activity, normally done toward the end of the project and by the personnel occupying leadership positions within the project organization.

What is wrong with this picture? Well, to begin with, if the project has fallen behind schedule and is over budget, the project team members that still remain in the project organization (have not been demobilized) are likely to be emotionally charged, stressed out, and frustrated by the situation. The customer is likely unsatisfied and wants to hear what went wrong, mostly so blame can be established and claims prepared. Everything is focused on what went wrong, and most people would have to rely on their memory of how events took place rather than reviewing facts. If managers alone participate in the lesson-learning session, *their* view on what went on, and not a balanced view of the project team, will be recorded as lessons.

A much more effective approach is to capture lessons on a daily basis as people use the system, make decisions, and introduce changes, and as organizations face staffing issues, as vendors are unresponsive, as project specifications are not present or are too conservative, as sponsors are not supporting the project, as stakeholders are mismanaged or are getting too gritty, as schedules seem short, or as budgets are insufficient.

It takes discipline to establish a culture where each work process is constantly evaluated for improvement while the related tasks take place.

A benefit of doing it this way is the ability to include everyone's input when it matters most—during or before the issue becomes a non-conformance, before inefficiencies are experienced, and potentially before mistakes are made, leading to rework.

If asked to identify the essentials for lessons to be truly learned, aside from following the above stated suggestions, I would say:

- *Effective communication:* Communication is the key to identifying the lesson with accuracy, arriving to a solution, preparing an adequate response, implementing actions, training personnel, and monitoring performance thereafter.

- *Team atmosphere:* Team atmosphere is difficult to achieve but easily lost when a blaming culture is established. The project team must learn to see quality issues as a learning mechanism. Preserving a team atmosphere will encourage individuals to continue bringing problems and issues to the table for everyone to cohesively work on, rather than hiding them to avoid blame and potential punishment.

- *Ownership, accountability, and integrity:* Work processes' ownership and accountability shall be established from the beginning. Integrity shall prevail at all times. A scarcity of lesson-learning occurs (and blame is more likely to result) when no one seems accountable for the affected work processes and subsequent repair of the system in the affected areas.

- *Trust and acceptance:* Trust that people are acting in good faith, and accept that things don't always go as planned or as expected.

- *Up and down approach (core business, system, work processes, procedures) with emphasis on work process improvement:* Each individual within the organization must contribute to learning, as lessons are expected to occur at different levels within the organization.

- *Encouragement and support by Management:* Management must walk side-by-side with others in the organization while implementing actions to rectify the causes of issues, problems, and undesired events. Management must be willing and able to allocate adequate funds for such actions— otherwise, lessons will not truly be learned, and more importantly, related issues, problems, and undesired events will recur.

- *The presence of a balanced and integrated system:* A robust and effective system shall be created and maintained. Whether it is called a Project, Quality, or Integrated Management System, the important thing is that it is complete, understood by all, and practiced under established governance.

Roberto Rodriguez Esteves

Continuous Improvement

A Continuous Improvement Process is a long-term approach that systematically seeks to achieve small incremental changes in work processes in order to improve efficiency, effectiveness, flexibility, and quality.

Key Concepts around Continuous Improvement, as presented in the book Kaizen: The Key to Japan's Competitive Success by Masaaki Imai, are:

- The purpose of a Continuous Improvement Process is the identification, reduction, and elimination of sub-optimal processes (efficiency).

- The core principle behind it is the (self) reflection of work processes through regular feedback by the users of such work processes (feedback).

- Emphasis is given to making incremental but continual improvement steps, rather than giant leaps (evolution).

Key features of Continuous Improvement:

- Improvements are based on many small changes.

- Small improvements are less likely to require major capital investment.

- Ideas come from both management and the workforce.

- All employees should continually seek ways to improve their own performance.

- Encourage workers to take ownership for their own work while also reinforcing team-work, thereby improving worker motivation.

More strategic elements include deciding how to increase the value of the product or service being provided to the customer (effectiveness), and how much flexibility is present to allow for change. Below are some recommendations:

- Aim to improve quality by working at the four levels in parallel (business/system, program, project/work process, and procedures).

- Develop a system around work processes (like the Flying Kite Execution Model).

- Establish and follow a "no-blame" approach toward quality issues.

- Build owner-contractor relationships through excellence of products and services (quality).

- Build the project organization based on performance, values, commitment, and teamwork.

- Perform regular detailed assessments on the maturity and effectiveness of system, programs, work processes, and procedures.

- Assure the implementation of action plans to achieve continuous improvement. Repeat the cycle over and over again.

- Bear in mind that quality of work is the one objective that cannot be sacrificed.

Roberto Rodriguez Esteves

Level	Target	Scope	Accountability	Guarantor
Business / System	Client Satisfaction and retention, System Improvement	Policies, Manuals, Strategic Plans, Systems, Tools	Executives and Directors	CEO/ Quality Director
Programs	Reduce Waste and Increase Benefits	Departments, Organization, Personnel, Work Processes	Designated Program Leads	V.Ps, Quality Director
Project / Work Process	Project Execution & Management, Work Process Improvement	Focus areas and related work processes	Project Managers and Process Owners	Functional Managers and Directors
Procedures	Documents and Templates that support the system	All standards, procedures, forms, templates, guidelines	Discipline Leads, Engineers, Users	Engineering Manager, PE, Quality Managers

Quality Improvement Levels

Table 4 - Quality Improvement Levels

Why is it that my kite won't fly?

Performance Indicators

Setting key performance indicators (K.P.I.'s) is not an easy task. I have been involved in setting up K.P.I.'s for projects, departments, and organizations. The S.M.A.R.T. methodology is perhaps the most effective way to formulate performance indicators that are meaningful and indicative of having achieved a true related mark. The letters in S.M.A.R.T. have the following meaning:

> **S** stands for specific: It should describe with detail and precision what is required. When used for objectives, it means that they should be clear, concise, and specific enough to provide direction.

> **M** stands for measurable: The associated achievement or progress can be measured.

> **A** could stand for either *assignable* or *achievable*: In other words, there always needs to be someone accountable for achieving the goals and objectives that support the K.P.I. Secondly, it means we should assign goals and subsequent K.P.I's that are challenging yet achievable.

> **R** could be used for relevant and realistic— realistic in the same sense of achievable, and relevant to the work process (s) and organization involved.

> **T** usually stands for time-based (time bound, timed, time-framed). It simply means that the related activities should have a time constraint that is both aggressive and realistic. This variable sets the period in which the evaluation for meeting performance will take place.

Let us explore how this would work on a day-to-day life example. Imagine that a friend of mine, John, would like to set up a K.P.I. around his commuting time and expenses to and from work:

John lives in the city of Calgary, Alberta, about twenty-five kilometers from his office. There are generally two routes (highway or streets) and several means of transportations (bike, bus, train, car) he could use to go to work. He's noticed that he seems to be investing too much of his valuable time and money commuting; he'd like to set a target to reduce his commute time each day by twenty minutes on average without having to move out of his house and while keeping his current job and potentially saving some money.

John currently takes his own vehicle to go to work and spends an average of $5,000.00 per year with an average round-trip duration of 120 minutes. Taking the train would be faster but is rather difficult after seven AM due to parking (most parking spots are taken by then); taking the bus is tough during the heavy winter months due to the cold. John works as per the company's flexible schedule policy, which allows him to come in at a reasonable time, so long as he puts 8 hours of work every working day..

He has committed to start measuring his commute time and cost on a daily basis, and to report it at the end of one year (240 working days).

Let us now place the performance indicator in S.M.A.R.T. form:

> *Specific:* To reduce John's commute time by twenty minutes per day on average, without having to move from his current house or leaving his current job, and while saving $2000 per year.

> *Measurable:* To be measured while using his watch, recording the time when he leaves his house and the time that he arrives at work (Time 1). Repeat this process when he returns home

(Time 2). Record the amount of time used for commuting on an Excel file. Time of commute (TC) = Time 1 + Time 2. Average commute time in a year = TC1 + TC2 + TC3 + … TC 240 / 240. Cost varies with the means of transportation used and is calculated as round-trip cost per day times the working days using that same mean of transportation, and then added to the other costs and divided by 240.

Assigned and achievable: This target is assigned to John. It is likely achievable provided strategies and discipline are exerted.

Relevant: He is looking to improve quality of life, so he wants to shorten his commute time to spend more time with his family and to exercise more frequently during the week.

Time-bound: Since John lives in a country with all seasons, the plan is to use a full year to arrive at the target. This is to allow for changes of weather that may affect commuting. Therefore, the exercise is bound to be done in a period of 365 days (240 working days).

Formulating a strategy requires lifting relevant information that could assist in performing the analysis. John is given five days to gather relevant information to prepare his strategy. Upon gathering information, the following data became available:

Roberto Rodriguez Esteves

Means of transportation	Trip duration - One way in minutes				Cost of round trip /day based on average duration, in $		Cost of round trip /day based on average duration, in $		Cost of round trip /year based on average duration, in $		Cost of round trip /year based on average duration, in $	
	Peak hours (7 to 8 AM and 4:30 to 5:30 PM)		Off Peak hours (before 7 AM and after 5:30 PM)									
	Spring-Summer	Fall-Winter	Spring-Summer	Fall-Winter	Spring-Summer	Fall-Winter	Spring-Summer	Fall-Winter	Spring-Summer	Fall-Winter	Spring-Summer	Fall-Winter
Bicycle	100	120	100	120	-	-	-	-	50.00	50.00	50.00	50.00
Bus	65	75	55	65	6.00	6.00	6.00	6.00	1,440.00	1,440.00	1,440.00	1,440.00
Train (including driving to train station and finding parking)	40	45	35	40	9.00	9.00	9.00	9.00	2,160.00	2,160.00	2,160.00	2,160.00
Own vehicle (includes gasoline at $12/100 KM on city and $9/100 KM on highway + parking at $15/day)	Highway				Highway	Highway	City	City	Highway	Highway	City	City
	55	65	45	55	19.50	20.63	21.00	22.50	4,680.00	4,950.00	5,040.00	5,400.00
	City											
	60	70	50	60								

Table 5 - Transportation's Cost and Duration -
Key Performance Indicators Example

John formulated a strategy to take different means of transportation during the year, to save both time and money. The table below shows the strategy followed:

Season	% Days	Split of Working Days	Transportation Means Taken									
			Bicycle	Bus peak hours	Bus off peak hours	Train peak hours	Train off peak hours	Vehicle peak hours city	Vehicle off peak hours city	Vehicle peak hours highway	Vehicle off peak hours highway
Winter	45%	108	0	0	8	0	40	0	30	0	30
Spring	10%	24	0	0	0	0	24	0	0	0	0
Summer	30%	72	10	0	40	0	12	0	0	0	10
Fall	15%	36	0	0	6	0	20	0	0	10	0
Total days at each transportation	100%	240	10	0	54	0	96	0	30	10	40
Subtotal Cost of transportation			$2.08	$0.00	$324.00	$0.00	$864.00	$0.00	$675.00	$223.44	$721.88
Total Cost of transportation in 1 year			$2,810.40								
Total savings in 1 year			$2,189.60								
Duration of round trip in hours			33.33	0.00	103.67	0.00	122.00	0.00	50.00	21.67	70.00
Total Commute Time in 1 year (in minutes)			24040								
Average commute time per day (in minutes)			100								

Table 6 - Action Plan -
Key Performance Indicators Example

Why is it that my kite won't fly?

John was able to reduce the average commute time to 100 minutes per day, while simultaneously saving $2,189.60. He did it with a combination of actions, which included taking different means of transportation, taking advantage of the both the weather conditions and the use of off-peak hours to avoid the heaviest traffic. Discipline was needed for John to work sixty-two days out of the 240 working days in an off-peak hours' schedule (personal sacrifice). An additional benefit was being able to incorporate ten days of commute by bicycle, adding some exercise to his busy life. At the end, he was able to spend more quality time with his family as well.

I know what you're thinking—the targets were set around Cost and Time, much like they would be set in project execution. Bear in mind, though, that despite those being the explicit targets, there are always hidden, not expressed, or otherwise expected to be maintained targets (expectations) which deserve equal attention. In the example given, it would make no sense that John's actions put in jeopardy his health, riding the bicycle in the colder days of the winter when temperatures fall below –20 F, though some people in Calgary do it. Nor would it be expected that in order to shorten his commute time, he would drive at speeds above the limits, increasing the risk of getting tickets or having an accident. Evidently, the strategy would have to get him to work at a reasonable time. No one said anything about productivity or quality of work. However, it is understood that the strategy should not lead to constantly being late, skipping important meetings, or working only six hours.

All of these things, expressed or not, form part of the requirements when setting key performance indicators. The expectation is that quality and safety in their broader sense are not sacrificed at the expense of fulfilling set targets.

Things to consider when setting up key performance indicators:

- Make them S.M.A.R.T.

Roberto Rodriguez Esteves

- They should be challenging and motivating.

- They should lead to continuous improvement of the related activities and work processes.

- The project team must have the discipline to measure and follow up. Otherwise, they could become a waste of time and be very demotivating.

- If missing the target, consider performing root cause analysis to determine if the target was too aggressive (optimistic), or other issues caused under performance.

- Assure that the indicators target to preserve (or improve) quality, safety, health, environment, team, motivation, functionality, and other deciding factors shared throughout the book.

When taking Quality as the holistic variable that allows us to manage everything in life well, it would appear that the K.P.I.'s could be drafted around assuring and improving the quality of products and services, together with the work processes that are used to realize them, and finally, how well we are managing those work processes. If we were to set our key performance indicators around the quality of products, services, work processes, and management during project execution, I suggest that the following areas of interest be covered in order to create a sufficiently good scenario for the project to succeed:

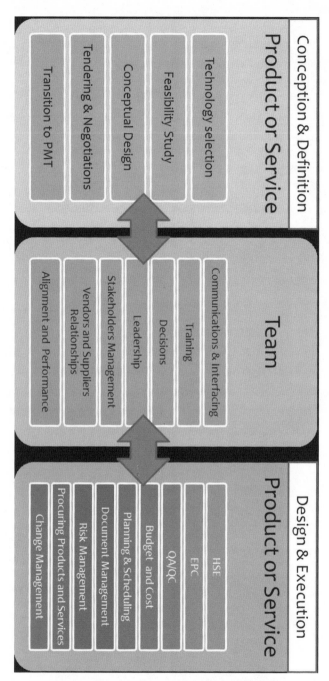

**Figure 15 - Assigning Key Performance
Indicators in Project Execution**

Chapter Eight: Integrating the Thoughts to Achieve the Desired Results

I have shared with you many concepts, ideas, and strategies to improve project performance. Before describing the Flying Kite Project Execution Model in detail, let's put some of these concepts, ideas, and strategies to the test by providing answers to typical problems encountered during my career in project management—problems that show up in audits, and problems that people share. The responses given are suggested solutions to the most common reasons for under-performing in Project Execution. Please remember that each project is unique; solutions that have worked in the past for some projects do not necessarily work when applied to a different one.

1. *Personnel are not qualified for the role*

   Measure competency levels and the existing gap, identify training required, train, coach, increase supervision, or eventually replace personnel. Seek help from functional managers and HR, as required.

2. *Unclear roles, responsibilities, and accountability*

   Improve description, define or clarify roles and responsibilities, and establish accountability for each work process.

Ensure orientation is given to each new project team member and refreshment of orientation program given to all project team members on a periodic basis. Validate understanding of responsibilities through adequate supervision of activities.

3. *Incomplete, missing, incorrect, or misleading procedures*

Revise, update, or re-write your project procedures to support proper execution of work processes. Use procedures to establish responsibilities around the work processes they are written for. Keep procedures to a minimum as too many of them can be overwhelming. Procedures not directly tied to a work process shall be eliminated. Re-orient focus to work processes.

4. *Scope was either not understood, incomplete, unexpressed, or overwhelming*

Improve scope verification process with the client and other stakeholders, including creating the necessary documentation. Apply change management for those areas that were left incomplete in previous phases of the project, particularly when no indication was given in the contractual documentation as being part of your scope of work. Document stakeholders' expectations.

5. *Client and stakeholders expectations were unclear, confusing, or unexpressed*

Create means for identifying, validating, and documenting expectations from the client and other stakeholders. Follow suggestions given in an earlier chapter of this book. Gather your team and discuss any punctual situation with stakeholders, and apply problem and conflict resolution, as required. Establish stakeholder management, if not done so already, aiming at improving relationships and meeting their expectations without compromising the project's outcome. If necessary, apply change management.

6. *Project requirements were unclear, misunderstood, unexpressed, not checked due to time constraints*

Create means for identifying, validating, and documenting contractual requirements. Make sure that proper time is allocated for performing this task. Utilize change management when expressed project requirements differ from contractual obligations. Review the Project Execution Plan (PEP) with your team to identify areas or disciplines where contractual requirements may not have been clearly understood and underperformance is anticipated.

7. *Schedule pressure: "There was no time for planning!"*

Working with unrealistic schedules actually requires more and better planning. Create the tools and work processes that allow for this activity to be properly performed. It may seem like a waste of time at first, but not having a plan to cope with a fast-track pace will likely cause more severe consequences. Apply change management when it is impossible to follow the current schedule and in order to increase the time given to major activities, especially critical path activities. Pay special attention to quality of products and deliverables. People will be working under pressure, thus will require increased supervision, better quality assurance, and prompt quality control. Resist to turning things in or delivering them to the client before the quality cycle has been completed.

8. *"Decisions made by others (including Management) impacted my work."*

Establish a sound decision-making process that includes making informed decisions, understanding impact on stakeholders, documenting decisions, and performing risk analysis around key decisions that could affect the outcome of the project. Measure the effectiveness of decisions after they have been implemented. Record with detail the consequences of past decisions, and if necessary, initiate change management to recover hours and money associated with changes that emerged from poor decisions. This could be internal change management if decisions did not include the client, or external otherwise.

9. *"External factors impacted my ability to perform my work to standards."*

Improve Risk Management to anticipate and have proper response plans for risks associated to external factors, namely: client changes, weather, laws and regulations, labor issues, etc.

10. *Negligence or poor attitude by personnel*

Investigate; coach and mentor personnel; improve communications; regularly measure motivation and morale levels; take action when needed to boost these variables. Exert leadership to show the way and provide guidance when so required. Disciplinary action may be required when no improvement is observed.

11. *Too short of a budget and/or contingency*

Apply change management. If no additional funds are granted, document expenditure for each project activity short of a budget. Make sure you have effective and well-documented work processes in place. Reinforce stakeholders (particularly client's) management to avoid scope creep, which would complicate things further. Once supporting documentation has been gathered, re-solicit adjustments to the project budget against real expenditure. Repeat this process for each area where budget seems insufficient, immediately upon completing the related activities. Other actions could be oriented to reducing the costs associated to the different project activities. These may include: negotiating purchase orders and contracts, improving productivity, reducing materials surplus, revisiting post-delivery equipment and materials handling strategy to avoid double-handling, among others.

12. *The quality of engineering deliverables is deficient*

Poor quality in engineering is usually caused by one of these factors: engineers working with the wrong or incomplete information, engineers amongst disciplines not talking to each other, engineering tools not fully understood or trained for, unrealistic shcedules, and change affecting finished products. To improve on the quality of engineering, supervisors and leads must ensure that the necessary and accurate data is available at the start of the design; personnel are trained in the use of the applicable tools; engineers are using the correct specifications with good understanding of the project specifications and other contractual requirements; multidisciplinary coordination is effective and done regularly. It is also suggested to perform a consistency check across disciplines upon finishing the major deliverables and before submitting the engineering packages to the customer. Bear in mind that fabrication and construction work that starts with deficient or incomplete engineering will likely be defective, and the cost to repair something once fabricated, installed, or built is three to ten times more expensive than fixing the associated engineering. Don't let pressure on meeting schedules be the prevailing factor that affects quality of engineering, because it will surely become the cause of project cost overruns as well.

Chapter Nine: Transcending Into a New Project Execution Culture

The Flying Kite Project Execution Model was borne out of an idea to improve project execution. Years of frustration at seeing mistakes repeat, years of data collection, attending formal and informal training, many work experiences, many success stories, a few failures, and an abundance of lessons were compiled to create this model.

This is a personal project that I started some seven years ago. It has taken me quite some time and much effort to put it together in some form that can be both understood and appreciated by others in the field of Project Management.

To put it into practice within any organization would require a mental shift. This shift would likely lead to a cultural shift for project management and execution, with a distinctive focus and a catching approach to ease its learning and facilitate its application. I like to think that many young professionals will benefit from having a tool that complements the many existing tools out there, with a unique approach to the delicate and complex subject of project management and execution. It's more than a tool—it's a model to learn, question, challenge, and improve upon. I welcome and encourage your thoughts.

So, to start, let me take you to the highest level within the structure of an organization (company or firm). All firms usually start
by defining their purpose, the reason for their existence, the
mission. They project the mission into the future and picture
how and where they see themselves in the not-too-distant future;
this is their *vision*. In order to get them to achieve their vision,
they would draft specific *objectives* (corporate objectives), which
would in theory get them to their ultimate goal in the desired
time frame. To make sure they can establish a corporate culture
that people can recognize as unique, which is hopefully practiced
by all employees as well, *values* must exist and must be shared
with everyone.

Underneath their mission, vision, objectives, and values lies
their system (or systems). This system integrates, in an effective and organized manner, the *policies, standards, work processes*, and *procedures* of the organization. *Tools* are selected
to assist employees in the fulfillment of their duties for gener-
ating the products and services produced by the organization.
Sustainable growth is achieved through the implementation of
programs and the execution of *projects*, with emphasis on continual improvement.

Take a few minutes to study the below diagram (Figure 16); it
integrates key concepts needed to support two of the eight
principles of Quality Management, namely, "Process Approach"
and "System Approach to Management". In the center of the
diagram are the work processes. Understanding the work processes is fundamental for executing the necessary tasks that
integrate to create the products and services described in the
mission statement.

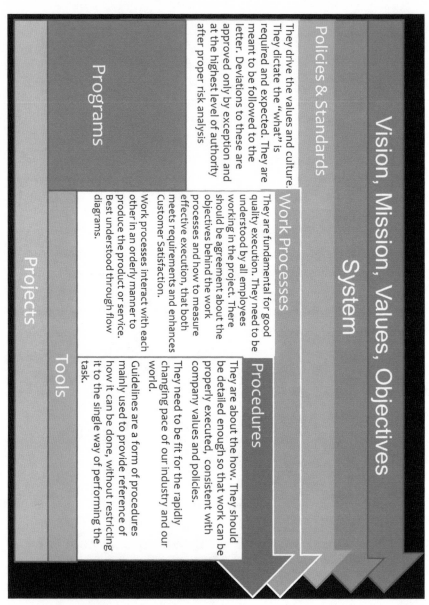

Vision, Mission, Values, Objectives

System

Policies & Standards

They drive the values and culture. They dictate the "what" is required and expected. They are meant to be followed to the letter. Deviations to these are approved only by exception and at the highest level of authority after proper risk analysis

Programs

Work Processes

They are fundamental for good quality execution. They need to be understood by all employees working in the project. There should be agreement about the objectives behind the work processes and how to measure effective execution, that both meets requirements and enhances Customer Satisfaction.

Work processes interact with each other in an orderly manner to produce the product or service. Best understood through flow diagrams.

Projects

Tools

Procedures

They are about the how. They should be detailed enough so that work can be properly executed, consistent with company values and policies.

They need to be fit for the rapidly changing pace of our industry and our world.

Guidelines are a form of procedures mainly used to provide reference of how it can be done, without restricting it to the single way of performing the task.

Figure 16 - The Structure of an Organization

You may be surprised to know that during several audits performed by me in different companies and project organizations, a number of employees were not able to identify the work processes used in their company to develop products and provide services. In a similar way, they struggled when asked, "What is the core business of the company you work for?" The immediate questions that came to mind were:

- How much of an orientation was given to these employees when joining the company?

- How could anyone expect employees to be effective and add value when unclear on the work processes required to perform their day-to-day activities?

- Is anyone doing anything to reverse this negative trend?

- How effective have the potential corrective actions been when it appears to recur year after year?

It was an eye-opener for me to try to come up with a system that would teach people about project execution. Project organizations should not have to rely on their orientation programs and a bunch of procedures to make it happen. This is rather ineffective, as discussed before. A system truly organized by work processes was urgently needed.

When we look at great operational systems created in the last twenty years, distinctive features include: being user friendly, being agile, accessible from anywhere, and being, as much as possible, self-taught.

There was one additional feature that I thought would complement this pack of features: the system needs to be capable of teaching anyone about project execution and management. The associated subjects usually require years of studying and practical experience in order to be learned. Thus, if the system were able to teach while you use it, then it would simplify having to orientate everyone, while also creating a consistent approach to project execution and management.

One last thing that is essential is developing a symbolic representation of the system. We memorize things better when we can incorporate several senses into it. A symbolic representation of the complex subjects of project execution increases the chances that the subjects will be learned (applying the principles of association in learning); once learned, people will tend to use it more frequently, thus the probability of developing a sustainable and effective working culture will emerge. The symbol chosen, as you by now would guess, is the Flying Kite. Having a symbol also aids communications, as people quickly learn the different components and can refer to them either in technical terms or in the representations given through the utilized symbols. In the next sections, I will explain the theory behind the symbol chosen and how it all integrates into an awesome project execution model.

Project managing and execution is like flying a kite, because:

- A person (the project manager) flies a kite (executes a project) of given characteristics in different ambient conditions (as per specifications and under certain conditions).

- He or she needs to be skilled at flying kites (skilled at managing projects).

- The kite will fly if there is sufficient wind (project justification and need).

- During the flight, there will be things that could bring the kite down, like strong winds, a storm, and an insufficient line (poor decisions, insufficient budget, change, poor planning, unresponsive suppliers, insufficiently-committed partners, cultural issues, local or regional regulations).

- The person flying the kite must overcome all of these adversities in order to continue flying it. (The project manager and its team must also overcome all kinds of adversities in order to complete the project with success.)

- Once steady, flying the kite is enjoyable and rewarding. (Well-planned projects with the right resources lead to successful project execution, and elevate the probability of having adequate responses to overcome whatever obstacles appear.)

- The person flying the kite always needs to be attentive to changes in weather and physical conditions, such as rain, lighting, wind, electrical lines, etc. (changes to client requirements and expectations).

- The stability of a flying kite is achieved by adding a tail. A sufficiently long and heavy tail would provide the kite with stability under severe ambient conditions. However, a tail that is too heavy may actually bring the kite down. (In project execution, quality is needed. Spending too much time on developing programs that take the products and services beyond standard quality and function may be too costly and time-consuming, making the project unviable.)

Flying a kite may be seen as a mix of art and science, so is *Project Execution*!

Another analogy to project management and execution was created from the kite. When taking the parts of a flying kite and comparing them to the different aspects of project execution, a direct correlation can be easily made. Below is a pictorial representation of a traditional flying kite for reference:

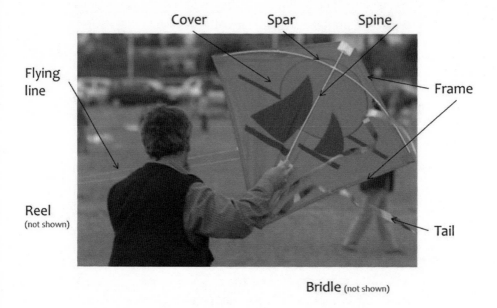

Cover Spar Spine

Flying line

Frame

Reel (not shown)

Tail

Bridle (not shown)

Figure 17 - Parts of a Flying Kite

Kite parts as they relate to project execution:

- *The frame*—the joined spine and spars, usually with a string connecting their ends, which form the shape of the kite and make a support for the cover. (*Mission, vision, values, policies, standards, business objectives.*)

- *The spar*—the support stick(s), which are placed cross-ways or at a slant over the spine. (*Initiation, execution and closure phases of a project.*)

- *The cover*—the paper, plastic, or cloth, that cover the frame to make a kite. (*Planning, control and assurance. Without them it is impossible to successfully execute a project*)

- *The spine*—the up-and-down or vertical stick that you build your kite around (*Transition from the definition phase to the execution phase of a project.*)

Roberto Rodriguez Esteves

- *The bridle*—one or more strings attached to the spine or spars, which help control the kite in the air. *(The project team grabs the project, like the bridle grabs the kite, creating balance and steadiness.)*

- *The flying line*—the string running from the kites' bridle, where you hold to fly the kite. *(The budget.)*

- *The tail*—a long strip of paper or plastic ribbons that helps to balance the kite in flight. *(The quality enablers.)*

- *The reel*—the object you use to wind your flying line to keep it from getting tangled or flying away. *(The project sponsors.)*

- *The pilot*—the person flying the kite. *(The project manager)*

The following picture captures the correlation made between a traditional flying kite and project execution. The use of a flying kite for developing my model for managing projects resulted out of how well the two items compare.

One of the most difficult things to do when flying a kite is to keep it balanced when it is hit by strong winds and unpredictable currents. A long and heavy tail creates balance and facilitates a stable flight. In project execution, the tail is equivalent to the quality enablers.

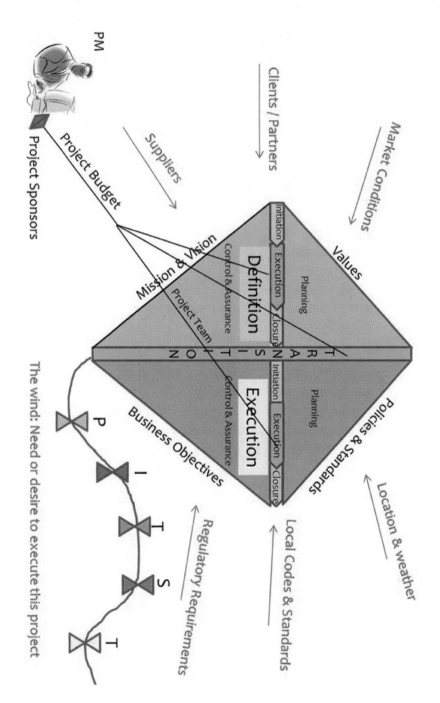

Figure 18 - The Flying Kite Project Execution Model

Roberto Rodriguez Esteves

An enabler is a facilitator. It is not imperative to execute the related activity (or activities), but it would sure help in executing such activity (s) with success (with quality, right the first time around, safely, etc.) The letters P.I.T.S.T indicate specific enablers that must be present for sound project execution, as follows:

- *People*—qualified, properly led, with common understanding of goals, knowledgeable about quality and project management, committed, motivated, working as a team.

- *Indicators for performance*—properly set up, leading to continuous improvement.

- *Training programs*—both general and specific to the task and related work process, planned for, documented, refreshed and based on latest and best practices.

- *System(s)*—work-process based, with clear accountabilities, agile, flexible and self-improving, while linking change, risk, communication, decisions, and stakeholder management.

- *Tools*—user-friendly, secured, effective, fast, and within economical reach.

A typical project organization would have its own Quality Management System. It is suggested to break it down to levels, almost as we were preparing a work breakdown structure of it in order to understand how it all works. This was a fundamental step for fixing the level at which the Flying Kite Project Execution Model was to be designed.

WBS of the Project Organization's Quality Management System

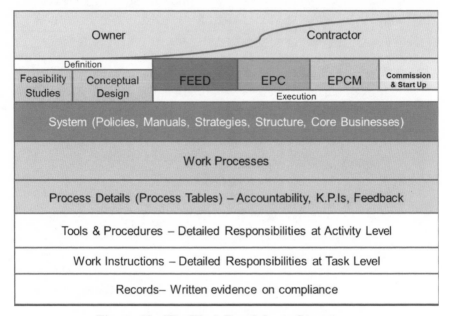

**Figure 19 - The Work Breakdown Structure
of the Flying Kite Model**

The focus is placed around "work processes". Thus the next step is to develop all the work processes required for project management and execution, and to organize the data in such a way that it can be systematically retrieved and learned with ease.

The figure below shows the right hand side of the kite, used to represent the execution phase of a project. A total of forty-eight work processes were identified and grouped in five categories (or execution phases), namely: *initiating, planning, executing, controlling and assuring, and closing.*

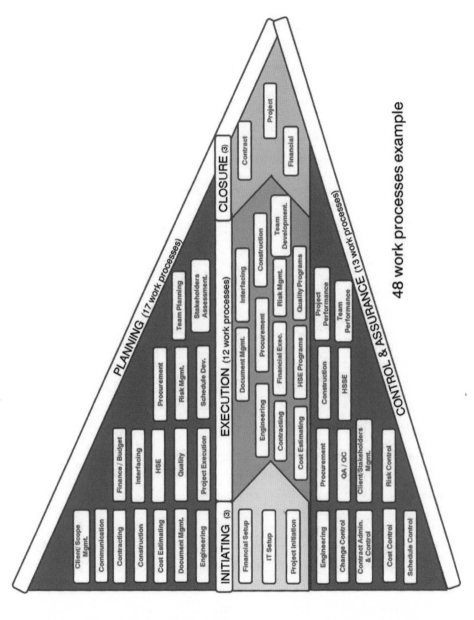

Figure 20 - The Execution Phase of a Project - Work Processes

The next step was to develop tables for each and every work process so people would have the information in a single place and could learn "the work processes". Accountability was established for each work process on a single individual within the project organization.

Key performance indicators (K.P.I.'s) were developed for each work process. The idea is to monitor performance at the work process level. If the project team is capable of fulfilling the requirements of each work process, measured against its own K.P.I.'s, the whole of work processes (the project) must be fulfilled as well.

Visibility on fundamental areas of management (decisions, communications, stakeholders, change, and risk) were added so management could systematically follow up on how these areas were managed by the project team.

Procedures, templates, and forms that were absolutely required for the execution of the related work process were added, so employees could access them directly from the system, in the most current electronic format.

Workflows were developed to facilitate forwarding of documents for review and approval. Once approved, these documents could be easily archived using the means created for work-process-project-specific archiving.

A feedback button was inserted to allow users to provide their comments on the use of the work process information and tools. Such feedback is directed to the work process owner and the quality assurance manager or director for processing (inclusion as is, corrective action, or whatever other action).

Work Process — Project Initiation

Accountability — Project Manager

Initiator	Input	Purpose	Output	Process Workflow	Procedures	Tools	End Users	Process Assets
Project Manager	- Signed Contract - Contractual Documentation - Preliminary Org. Chart and Mobilization Plan - High level schedule	To get the project underway and set up for success. It involves the creation/approval of the following documents: -Risk Matrix -Communication Plan -Stakeholders analysis It also requires the setup and opening the following: -Decision Log, Change log, Risk Register	- Project Charter - Project Kick Off Meeting Minutes - Project Initiation Checklist - Risk Matrix - Communication plan - Stakeholders Analysis - Decision log - Change log - Risk Register	Process Workflow #3	- Effective Kick Off meetings - How to develop a Project Charter - Initiation Checklist Procedure	N/A	- Project Sponsors - Clients - Project Team - Other stakeholders	The greatest asset is to have a charter to plan and execute the project accordingly. Secondly, to share objectives with everyone

K.P.Is
1- Documented Project Initiation Session
2- Signed as approved and distributed Project Charter
3- Completed and approved Project Initiation Checklist

Decisions | Communications | Risks | Changes | Stakeholders

Figure 21 - A typical Work Process Table within the Flying Kite Model

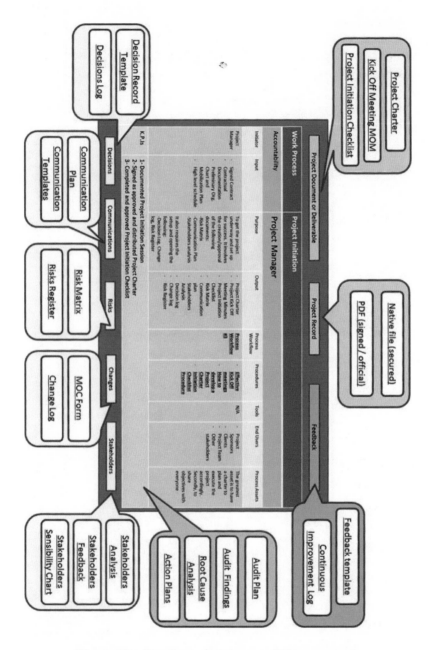

Figure 22 - Fundamental Areas of Management, Documentation, & Feedback for a Typical Work Process

Roberto Rodriguez Esteves

After each and every work process table has been completed, the system is checked across work processes to establish interrelations, check for consistency and governance requirements. This is to ensure that the Systems Approach to Management principle is accomplished.

Voilà—a system for project management and execution has been created!

The Flying Kite Project Execution Model is robust, complete, and has been assembled while using the latest software application technologies. It is a great tool to learn from, work against, and improve performance. It is fully adaptable to any type of project, any industry, and has been designed to suit most project organizations.

My two cents worth on cost and schedule control

Cost and schedule control should be treated like any of the other work processes. Do them well, with care, and while fulfilling their specific key performance indicators. Schedules and budgets are our best estimation of what a project should last and cost. Paying too much attention to cost and schedule pushes project teams to work to meet them at all expense, which has direct consequences not only on quality, but safety, integrity and completeness of design, relationships, motivation levels of personnel, and ultimately may cause a negative impact on the overall project performance.

For years, people have made too much of a correlation between project management and cost and schedule management, almost as if these were the only important variables. With all due respect for project sponsors, shareholders, and alike: if truly wanting to improve project performance, we should expand our horizons and think outside the box, which ultimately means paying more attention to other equally important variables and processes, which could drive costs and schedules off.

A contributing factor to the importance we give to time and money is how we have been brought up. What we have learned at school or in the early part of our lives determines the variables that we give more importance to. Society, particularly when living under a capitalist system, teaches us to see money as the most important variable, because without money we've got nothing. Money becomes the focus. Everything is about earning money so we can obtain what we want. But what we want is not always what we need. Societies also teach us time. The emphasis over taking time seriously starts at school, as well as in sports, piano classes, and college, and carries on through our working lives. Yes, time is money, so use it wisely, say our elders.

When and how do we learn about *quality, risk, communication, change, decisions,* and *stakeholders*? Wouldn't it be nice if some of these subjects were taught at our schools from our early years? The fact is that most of us learned about *quality* when we bought something which did not have it, and it turned out to be a fiasco. We probably learned about *risk* when we exposed ourselves beyond what we would have as adults, likely jumping into waters which we did not know, riding our bikes in the middle of the street and crossing intersections at high speeds without looking for incoming traffic. We generally don't see *communication* as a subject until we reach college. How are we supposed to be good at communicating while not understanding the basics? Perhaps we learned about *change* when we had to move to a new community because Dad had transferred jobs; we learned to adapt to a new school, a new set of friends, etc. We learned about good and bad *decisions* probably when we got spanked by our moms the first day we skipped school, or did something that we were not supposed to do. And the least visible subject throughout is *stakeholders*. It's cost us a lot of fights, a few tears, and a couple of black eyes to understand that things have stakeholders, and that sometimes there are stakeholders who can appear all of a sudden and claim to have interest or even rights over something we have or are working on. Most likely, society did not teach us to deal with stakeholders in the same sense as you do in project execution.

It is not unusual, then, that people would focus their attention on what they are good at, and what they have been taught for years to keep an eye on: time and money. If you were born from a low-middle class family, like me, though, you would know that money is not easy to come by; you would value the pair of dressing shoes that Mom and Dad had given you, because it was probably the only pair you would receive in a full year. You would not dare be so stupid as to risk damaging your shoes while playing on the ground in the rain (*risk*). You would find ways to politely excuse yourself from playing without being exposed to ridicule by your peers (*effective communication*). You would probably take better care of your shoes by cleaning them often (*preserving their quality and integrity*). You'd understand it would be a while before you got another pair, usually when you had outgrown them, so change was out of the question at least until wear and tear made them almost impossible to wear (*change*). It would be up to you to take care of your shoes, as Mom and Dad would clearly state when buying them. The consequences of good or poor decisions around the use of your shoes would become your lessons on decision-making and being responsible or not (*decisions*). There would basically be two stakeholders: your parents and you, unless you happened to have a brother or sister who wore the same size as you and could occasionally borrow or lend. Mom and Dad would be the sponsors and thus would be affected if having to replace your shoes earlier than expected. Your sibling would be a stakeholder if able to borrow the shoes. You would be the main stakeholder because you would pay the consequences on damaging your shoes too early. For sure, you would spend time warning your sibling to take care of your shoes!

The above example shows that you can be aware of time and money, yet be focused on quality, risk, communications, change, decisions, and stakeholders.

The years of playing with productivity factors to justify delays, increasing labor force at construction sites beyond reasonable density to try to expedite construction, cutting corners, expediting the beginning of fabrication or construction to accommodate schedules despite not having progressed enough in engineering, and other ineffective measures that try to correct rather than prevent, are over.

Consistently effective project execution lies on adequate planning and lots of attention to the people that are making it happen. Change will shadow us no matter how fast we run. The risk of not resulting as planned is there and shall be managed, including dealing with the consequences of inaccurate estimating of both project costs and duration. Quality is the mother variable and shall be treated as a value.

Whether it is the Flying Kite Project Execution Model, or whichever other model that your project organization decides to follow, make sure it truly leads to successful project execution, or do something to fix it. Be proactive and caring, if not for the company that you work for, for yourself and for those who follow.

Let us all work toward reversing the current trend of project execution failure and create the scenario for success. It is totally possible!

Chapter Ten: The Quest to be Inspiring and Extraordinary

We can work hard for years as project managers but may not get too far unless we excel at two things: mastering self-leadership and getting results while working with average teams. I don't claim to be a master of either of the two, but have had some success at it, in part because of the way I am (visionary, organized, disciplined, methodical, outgoing, not afraid to ask or say *I don't know*, friendly, humble, caring, ethical, honest, and straightforward).

I dedicate these last sections of the book to sharing my knowledge on these two subjects, with the hope it sparks your interest. If, after reading it, you too start your journey for the inspiring and extraordinary, I will have accomplished my objective.

The importance of mastering self-leadership

Do you want to be a good leader? What do you think is required? Are you doing what it takes to get you there?

There are many types of leaders; some are more inspirational than others. The reasons could vary, but one that comes to mind is that some leaders are able to balance their lives to the point that they can exert leadership in several areas of influence, while others focus on a single area of influence, leaving other areas unattended.

My interest on the subject of self-leadership and learning how to live a "balanced life" started during the '90s when I attended a training session on Emotional Leadership. The instructor explained that in order to reach one's own full potential and be happy, one needed to achieve and maintain balance among the five critical areas of life. These critical areas were *family*, *health*, *work*, *spirit* and *community*.

The number one obstacle in achieving such balance is *time*, and the number one enemy is *yourself*. We easily and frequently find ourselves procrastinating about things that we need to do in order to achieve our own goals; we postpone that important meeting with a loved one to resolve a past incident; we spend numerous hours on a single activity (Facebook, work, etc.) while unfulfilling other equally-important needs and demands.

Self-leadership is defined as "the process" of influencing oneself to establish the self-direction and self-motivation needed to perform.[2] The order of things is, in my opinion, as follows:

- Good leaders are able to practice self-leadership

- Self-leadership requires time management

- Time management requires awareness, self-discipline, planning, and control

A work/personal-life balance is not easily achieved. Society seems to be moving toward a faster pace each year; longer work hours, more commuting time, and more time in front of the computer consume our days. People devote more and more time to a single critical area—*work*. So, what happens to the rest of the critical areas? What are the potential consequences?

- Trouble with your spouse, leading to a divorce

---

2 *Self-Leadership: Leading Yourself to Personal Excellence* by Christopher P. Neck and Charles C. Manz

- Overlooking strange behavior by your teenager, which could lead to them engaging in drug addiction, and other more severe consequences

- Kids under-performing in school

- Health issues due to stress, lack of exercise and sleep, poor diets, etc.

- Unattended communities, higher crime rates, more pollution

- People losing respect for others and anti-values kicking in

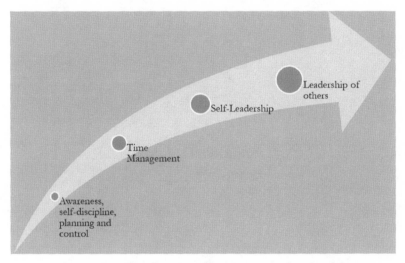

Figure 23 - The Road to Excellence in Leadership

This same instructor of the Emotional Leadership training session taught us to think of life as if you were a juggler who is so good that you are able to juggle five balls at once while running through time. Four balls are made of glass and one is made of rubber. You can only afford to drop the one made of rubber, because if you were to drop any of the other ones, they will break (severe consequences). The ball made of rubber was *work*. He said that no matter how bad it may seem to lose a job or to have to transfer to another company because you could not stand the working environment of the one where your were, you could always bounce back and in a few months be back on track with your professional goals.

The moral of the story is this: Work intelligently and responsibly. If you find yourself working long hours all of the time, chances are you may be leaving little time for the other critical areas (balls made of glass), which in the long run may cause undesired consequences.

Figure 24 - Balance in Life

After hearing this, I looked back to see if I'd had any such experiences—and I had indeed, well before attending this Emotional Leadership training session. In fact, I had already experienced the consequences of not balancing life at least twice.

I spent a few years living in Hawaii, U.S.A. back in the 1990s. I had set myself up to legally obtain my residence visa and remain in the U.S.A. with my family. I worked hard and for long hours for two consecutive years with a temporary working visa, until finally the moment I had been waiting for arrived. I was contacted by the embassy of the United States out of Caracas, inviting us to go pick up our residence visa and re-enter the country as immigrants. At about the same time, and due to many problems including a difficult economic situation, lack of time together because I was always working, excessive stress caused by the distance, and the need to provide care for our child, my wife and I started to experience serious problems. A few months after obtaining the resident visa, my wife decided she was going back to Venezuela with the child. I felt that my world was falling apart. After wanting something so much and finally receiving it (the visa), I had to let it go if I wanted to see my child grow. Work had prevailed and the glass ball (my marriage and family) had fallen and broken in pieces.

I look back today and realize that despite getting smashed against the wall and losing my marriage during what I would call my first major fault at keeping balance in my life, I had not learned the lesson.

About twelve years later, I had remarried and had built a family again. I found myself working long hours on a job that required about forty-five minutes of commuting each way, every day. I used to leave the house at around 5:45 am in order to make it to work by 6:30 am. Long hours, traffic, and other things again got in the way of creating balance, spending quality time with the kids and my wife, socializing, exercising, meditating, etc. After about two years into the job, I fell with a health issue. My back was strained beyond the limits due to sitting for long hours and getting little exercise. I spent thirty continuous days with lumbago, defined as pain in the lumbar region of the back, which could be caused by several factors including injury, back strain, arthritis, abuse of the back muscles (such as from poor posture, a sagging mattress, or ill-fitting shoes), or any of a number of other disorders. This tragic and painful moment of my life led to surgery to stabilize my lower back.

This time around I learned the lesson. I promised I would change the way I approached life and would reorganize my priorities with consideration to what I had learned. It took me two major incidents, lots of pain, and quite severe consequences to finally take balance seriously.

Hopefully you still have time to act and create balance in your life before you may have to experience similar undesired consequences.

Working with an "A Team" versus an "Underdog Team"

I love team sports! It is absolutely fascinating to see all that energy, skill, and strategy converted into the excitement that sports brings to our lives. Competition has been around for a long time; there have always been teams who succeed and those who fall short of meeting their goals. Why?

Physical and mental preparation, technique, practice, experience, motivation, and commitment make a great deal of difference for those teams who consistently make it to the playoffs and win tournaments.

The most successful franchise in professional baseball, the New York Yankees, have won forty World Series. The closest competitor, the San Francisco Giants, have done very well in the last five years by winning three times; they have a total of twenty wins overall. That is half the amount of wins by the Yankees.

The Yankees have been quite successful, but some attribute it to their payroll. When it comes to payroll, they have generally carried the highest payroll in the business. In 2013 they had a payroll of $229 million versus only $58 million carried by the Tampa Bay Rays, who finished second in their division ahead of the Yankees and behind the world champions, the Boston Red Sox with a payroll of $151 million. Is payroll the most influencing factor? Well, if we see it as their profession, in theory, players who earn more money should do more. After all, they get those big bucks because they are consistently outstanding.

Roberto Rodriguez Esteves

The Championship Coaches Network (Jeff Janssen, Janssen Sports Leadership Center) describes sports teams as being one of the following:

> "*Underdog*—on paper, your team appears to have little chance of succeeding because of a sub-par regular season record. Most often this is because you have less talent than your opponents, but could also be due to injuries, youth, and/or inconsistent play. Whatever the case, as football coach Bill Parcells once said, 'You are what your record says you are.' In this case, you are an 'underdog,' and few people expect you to have much of a chance, perhaps even some of your athletes.
>
> *Up and Comer*—your team has a solid level of talent and you are looking to break through to the next level and contend for a championship. Many programs get to this level but then come up against a perennial dominant program and have a hard time mentally and physically overcoming them.
>
> *Top Dawg*—your team is one of the clear favorites to win. Expectations are high and you are the team that everyone else is trying beat. You likely have a highly talented team and a great regular season record going for you, but now you must perform under the pressure of the playoffs."

For some reason, there is nothing more exciting than to watch an underdog team make the playoffs—and much more winning a World Series! The kind of connection automatically generated with fans grows quickly. Inspiration is contagious! The more you watch how the events unfold, the more driven you feel to celebrate and even claim as your own victory, because *you believed* when many did not.

Now, imagine this same phenomenon at a working organization. Imagine for a moment two project teams within the same corporation competing for resources, where one gets most of the "A" type professionals, while the other gets whomever is left. This happens more often than you think in organizations. Corporations need to meet today's ever-demanding standards, which implies keeping organizations flat and overhead costs under control. It is not uncommon to see excessively-reduced staffing levels with a greater work load for everyone.

Organizations also compete for the best professionals, with the clear advantage belonging to those who can afford such professionals (just like the New York Yankees).

This is the time when highly-skilled managers are required—managers who are capable of taking an underdog team and making it a success story. But what would that entail?

> "As an Underdog, you'll have some real challenges on the physical and mental fronts. Your biggest challenge is likely that you just don't have the talent necessary to compete. Further, from a mental standpoint, your team likely doesn't have much confidence and belief based on the negative results from the regular season. Your team may be pessimistic about its chances and may be ready for the whole season to end. Finally, you'll likely be on the road for all of the playoffs and you may have waning parent and fan support. Realistically, this is not a great situation to be in on the surface, but there can be hope if you frame it right."
> —*Jeff Janssen, Janssen Sports Leadership Center.*

As a project manager, your role is to lead your team to accomplish the goals and objectives that have been given to you. It requires a whole lot of focus, strategy, and commitment to be able to do it with a team of professionals who have not been very successful in the past.

Through the years, I have had the opportunity to succeed at working with underdog teams or underdog individuals. Such individuals or teams usually have the same desire as anyone else to succeed. Sometimes all it takes is caring and strategizing to make the big difference. I started to think of what worked for me in the past, and managed to compile it into six steps:

1. *Perform deep analysis.* Meet with your team members on an individual basis. Identify weaknesses and strengths, describe project goals, and talk about the obstacles they see in achieving them. You have to know with as much detail as possible who you have on your team, as well as their past successes and defeats. Apply root cause analysis to try to identify why things did not go well last time around. *Listen and analyze.*

2. *Make them believe* (individually and as a team). It is crucial to describe a positive outcome where they are the leading actors. Be inspirational, be convincing, and show them how you will be there to help them make it a reality. Don't be afraid to identify team weaknesses, but focus on placing the attention around team strengths and building from them. *Build trust.*

3. *Strategize to the greatest detail possible.* Prepare for the challenge. You must have the ability to project a winning image that is supported by a clear and sound strategy—a strategy that is constructed as a team with your leadership, making it embraceable. Make it a strategy of hard work and commitment, which will pay off for all. *Engage and generate commitment.*

4. *Perform with presence.* Communicate; drive; encourage; communicate; drive; encourage some more. Underdog teams may lack competency and your goal is to elevate their competency level. They may lack self-esteem and your goal is to inject it in their veins. *Be there!*

5. *Celebrate small triumphs.* Continue to motivate. Don't wait until the end to celebrate. Small steps reached deserve attention and can be used as great examples to keep it up. If anyone makes a mistake or if an activity falls behind, correct it and pick up the pace. Stay positive and encouraging. *Build esteem and assurance.*

6. *Watch events evolve and intervene only as needed.* Once momentum and high performance are achieved, intervene only when needed; observe and coach. Don't micro-manage. The idea is to help them be effective teams, not for you to be the team with their help. *Let them play.*

Many managers prefer to work only with the best. The sacrifices of working with an underdog team are overwhelming for them. However, to take an underdog team and make it a winner can be much more gratifying *for both you and the team!*

In closing

I sincerely hope you've enjoyed reading this book. Whether you're new to Project Management or already a seasoned professional, there are challenges ahead which you cannot afford to ignore. The typical causes of project failure will not disappear by themselves. Rather than adding to the negative statistics, you have a brilliant opportunity to be part of the solution. Whether you decide to adopt the methodologies shared in this book, or prefer to draft your own, the important thing is to commit to finding ways to reverse the current trend of unsuccessful project execution, and continue to make project management a career of choice.

Happy project execution!

Printed in Canada